Editor
Sara Connolly

Cover Artist
Marilyn Goldberg

Editor in Chief
Ina Massler Levin, M.A.

Creative Director
Karen J. Goldfluss, M.S. Ed.

Art Production Manager
Kevin Barnes

Mazes Design & Imaging
Rosa C. See

Publisher

Mary D. Smith, M.S. Ed.

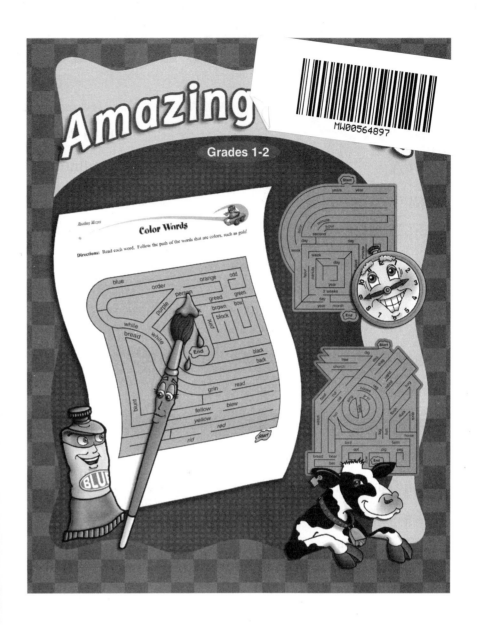

Grades 1-2

Color Words

Directions: Read each word. Follow the path of the words that are colors, such as gold.

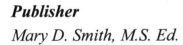

Author

Debra J. Housel, M.S. Ed.

Teacher Created Resources, Inc.
6421 Industry Way
Westminster, CA 92683
www.teachercreated.com

ISBN: 978-1-4206-5986-3

©2008 Teacher Created Resources, Inc.
Reprinted, 2012
Made in U.S.A.

Teacher Created Resources

Table of Contents

Introduction

Mazes date back at least 4,000 years to the time of Greek myths. In Roman times, mazes and labyrinths were found in artwork and in the design of floors in homes and public buildings. At that time, mazes were not considered puzzles. They were considered an artform.

Parents and teachers may underestimate the use of mazes in teaching and reinforcing skills in children. Mazes are not just fun activities; there are educational benefits for developing young minds in negotiating and mastering a maze.

Mazes strengthen

- hand-eye coordination
- fine motor skills (shoulder to wrist to hand)
- spatial sense
- deductive reasoning skills
- problem-solving skills
- logical-thinking skills

Best of all, students are developing all these skills in an entertaining way! Plus, the puzzles in *Amazing Mazes* provide even greater educational value because they ask students to use developmentally appropriate reading or mathematical knowledge. An answer key is provided at the end of the book.

Mazes can be tricky for beginners, so it is important to demonstrate how they are done. Do one or two mazes of each type (reading and math) together before expecting your students to be independent. Suggest that children first trace the potential path with their fingers before using a pencil. This promotes planning skills and reduces erasing.

Use these suggestions to get the most educational benefit from these mazes:

- have students cross out all incorrect responses before finding their way through the maze
- have students highlight all correct responses before finding their way through the maze
- for reading mazes, have students make an alphabetical list on another sheet of paper of all the words that met the criteria set forth in the maze (for example, *words with a long E sound*)
- for math mazes, have students write a related definition at the bottom (for example, define *chronological order* or *odd number* in your own words)

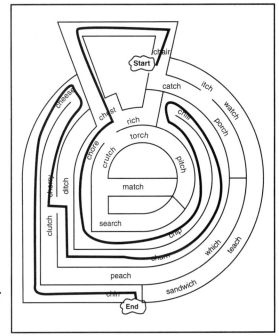

The best quality of these mazes is the enjoyment experienced by the user as he or she solves them. Your students will have fun while actively engaged in reinforcing knowledge. In addition, completing the mazes successfully will give children a sense of accomplishment and self-confidence.

Short A

Directions: Read each word. Follow the path of the words that have a short *A* sound as in *man*.

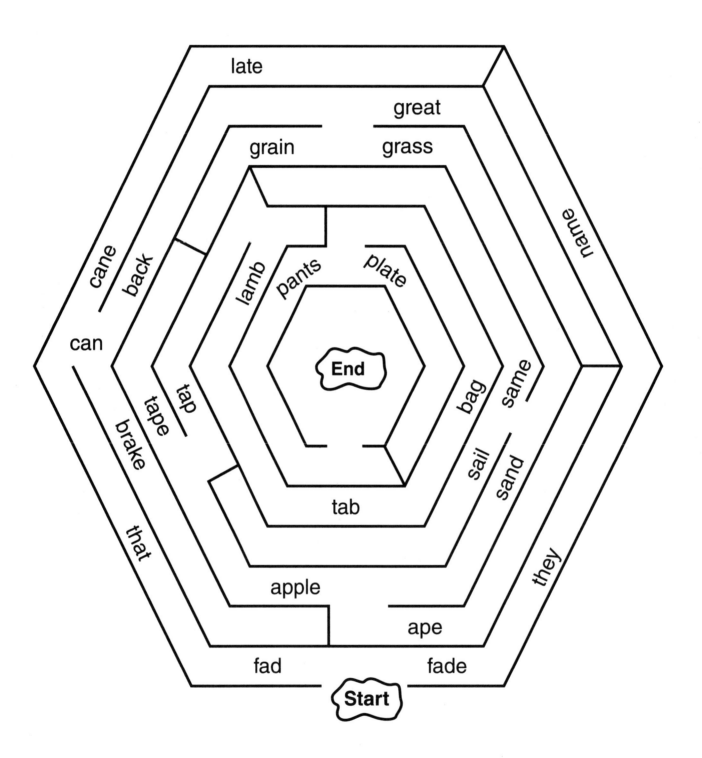

4

Long A

Directions: Read each word. Follow the path of the words that have a long *A* sound as in *rate*.

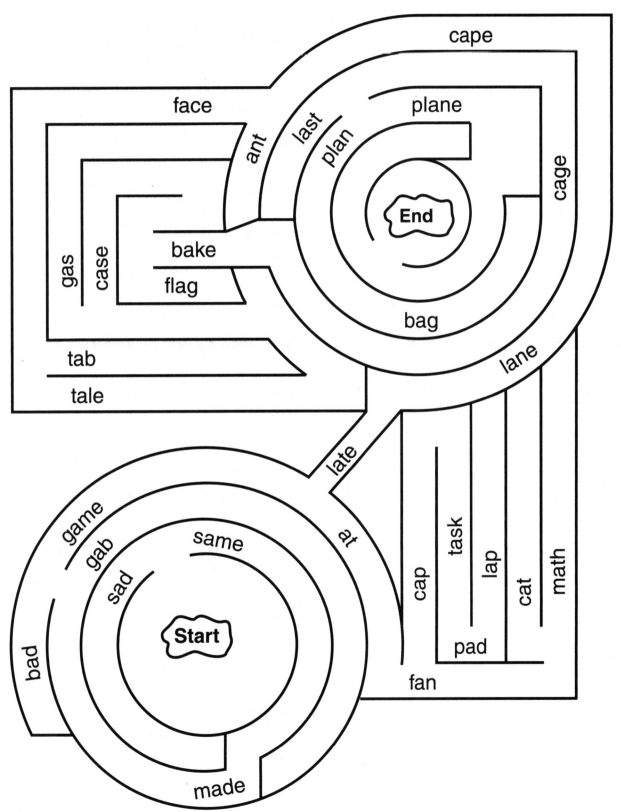

Short E

Directions: Read each word. Follow the path of the words that have a short *E* sound as in *met*.

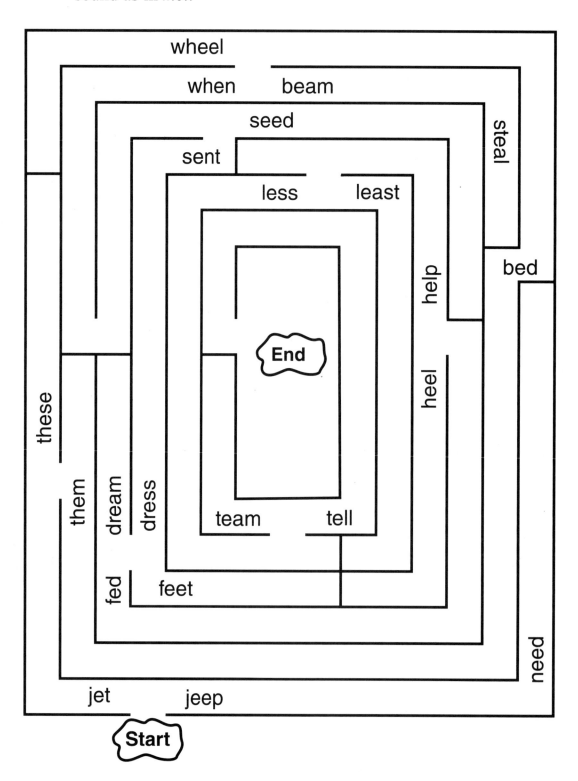

wheel

when   beam

seed

steal

sent

less   least

bed

help

these   End

heel

them dream dress

team   tell

fed feet

need

jet   jeep

Start

6

Long E

Directions: Read each word. Follow the path of the words that have a long *E* sound as in *me*.

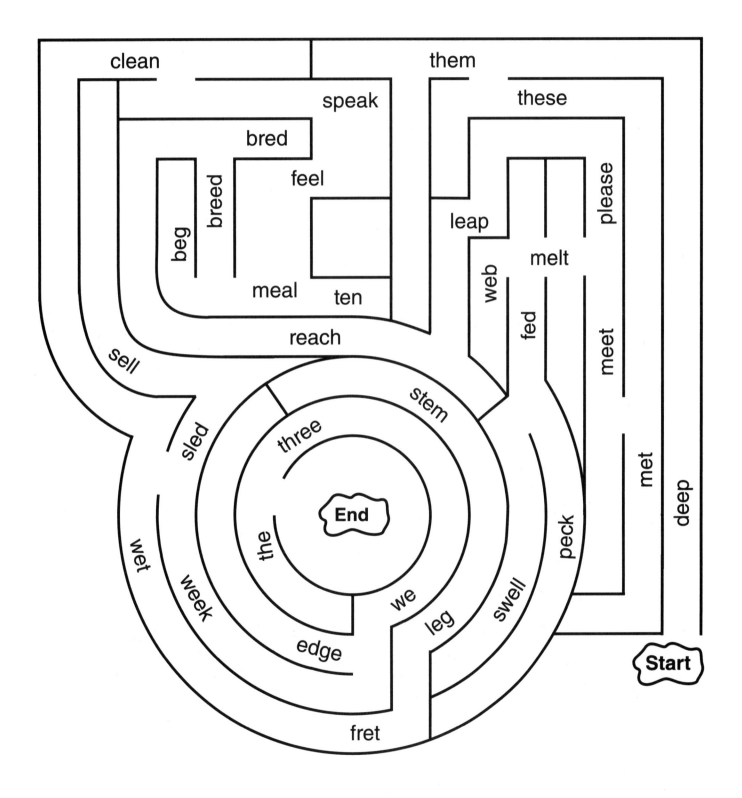

Short I

Directions: Read each word. Follow the path of the words that have a short *I* sound as in *sit*.

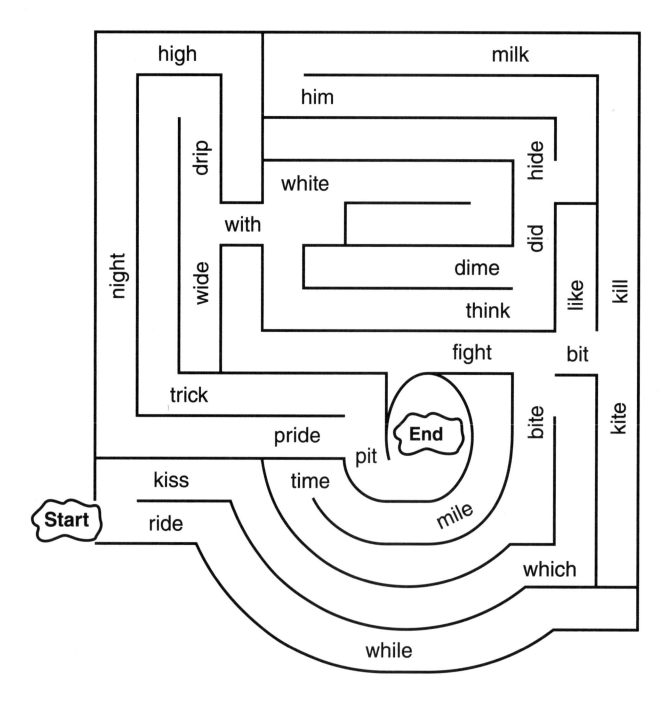

8

Long I

Directions: Read each word. Follow the path of the words that have a long *I* sound as in *bite*.

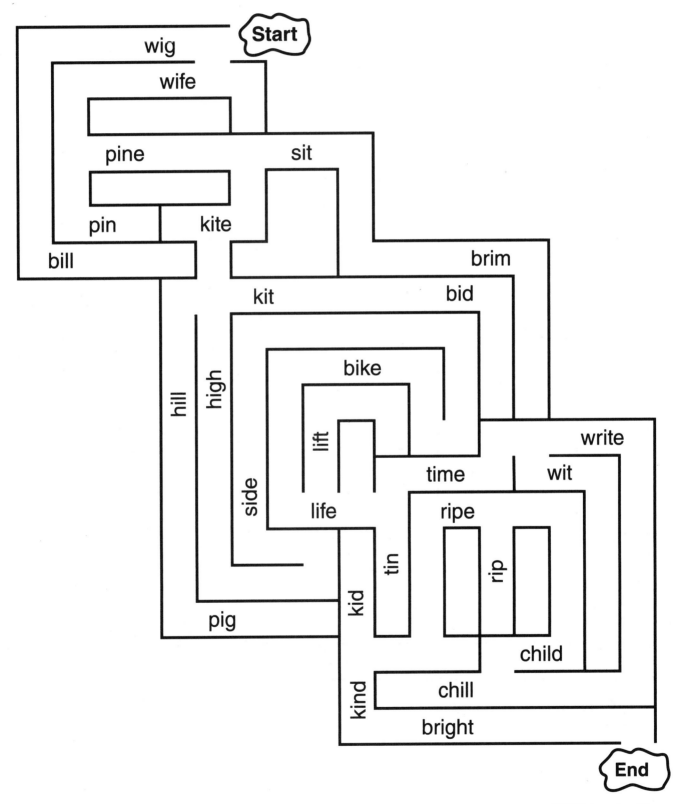

Short O

Directions: Read each word. Follow the path of the words that have a short *O* sound as in *sob*.

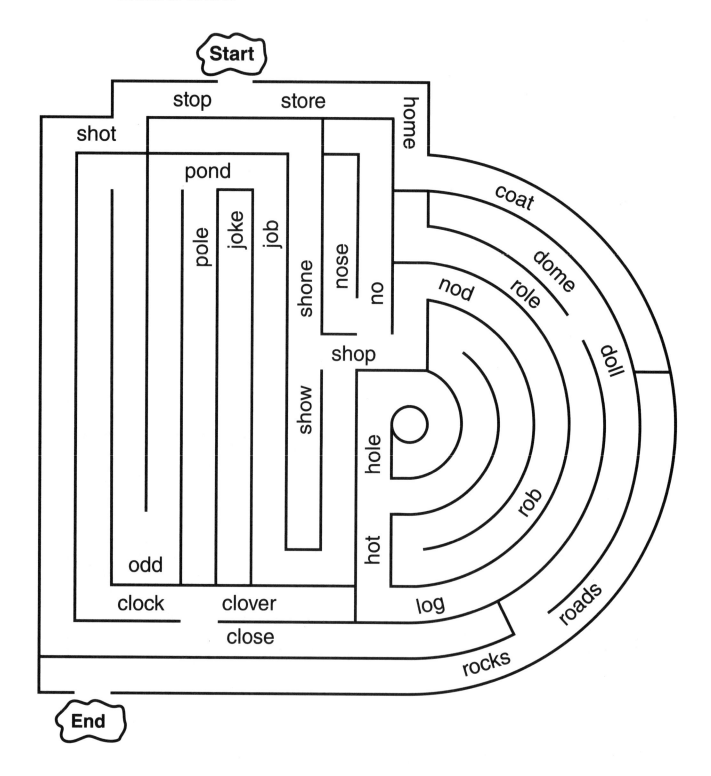

Long O

Directions: Read each word. Follow the path of the words that have a long *O* sound as in *boat*.

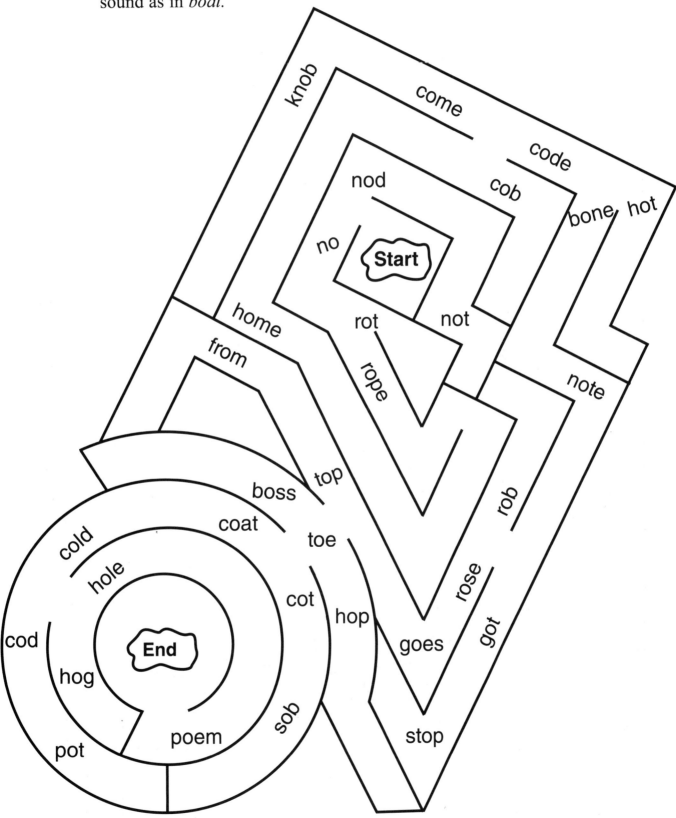

knob · come · code · nod · cob · bone · hot · no · Start · rot · not · home · rope · note · from · top · boss · coat · toe · rob · cot · hop · rose · got · cold · hole · cod · End · hog · goes · rose · stop · pot · hog · poem · sob · stop

Short U

Directions: Read each word. Follow the path of the words that have a short *U* sound as in *cut*.

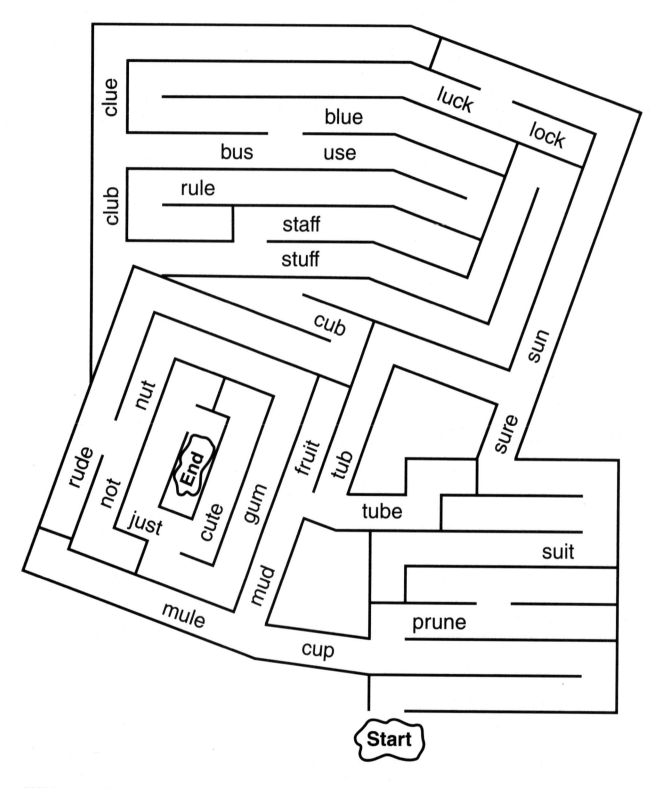

Long U

Directions: Read each word. Follow the path of the words that have a long *U* sound as in *mule*.

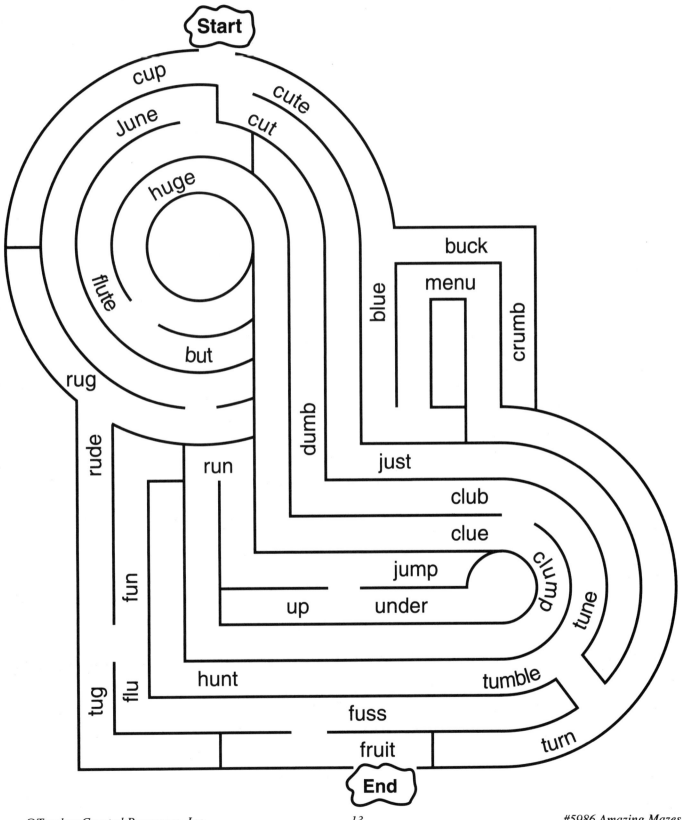

Start

cup

cute

June

cut

huge

blue

buck

menu

crumb

flute

dumb

just

but

rug

club

clue

rude

run

clump

tune

fun

jump

up

under

tug

flu

hunt

tumble

fuss

turn

fruit

End

Y is a Consonant

Directions: Read each word. Follow the path of the words in which *Y* is a consonant (such as *yellow*).

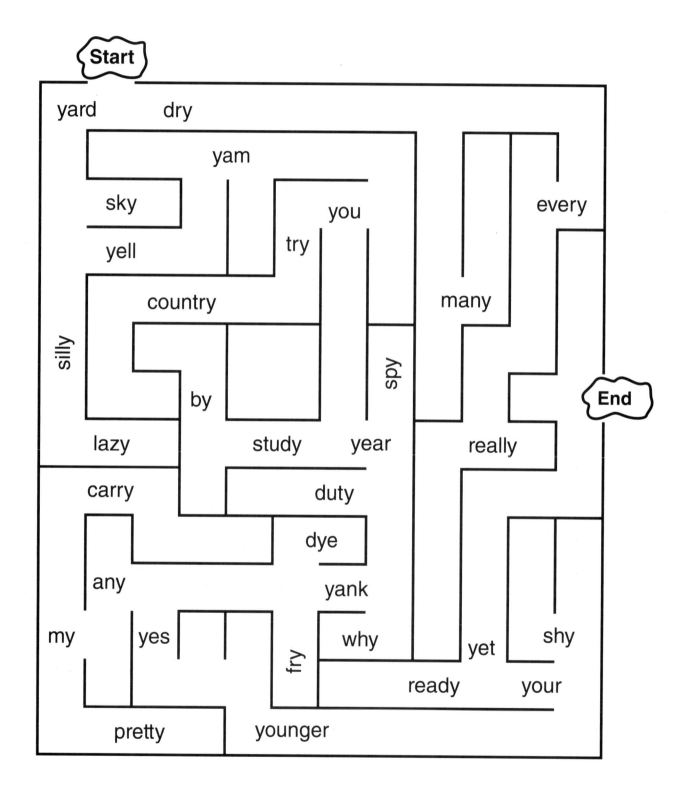

Y is a Vowel

Directions: Read each word. Follow the path of the words in which *Y* is a vowel (such as *try*).

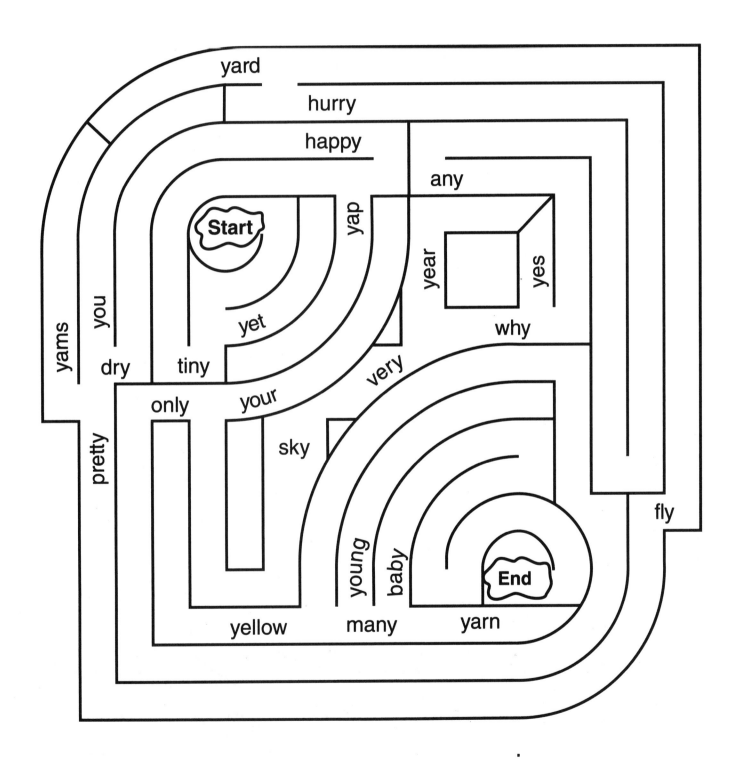

Letter Pair: CH

Directions: Read each word. Follow the path of the words that begin with the *ch* sound as in *cheer*.

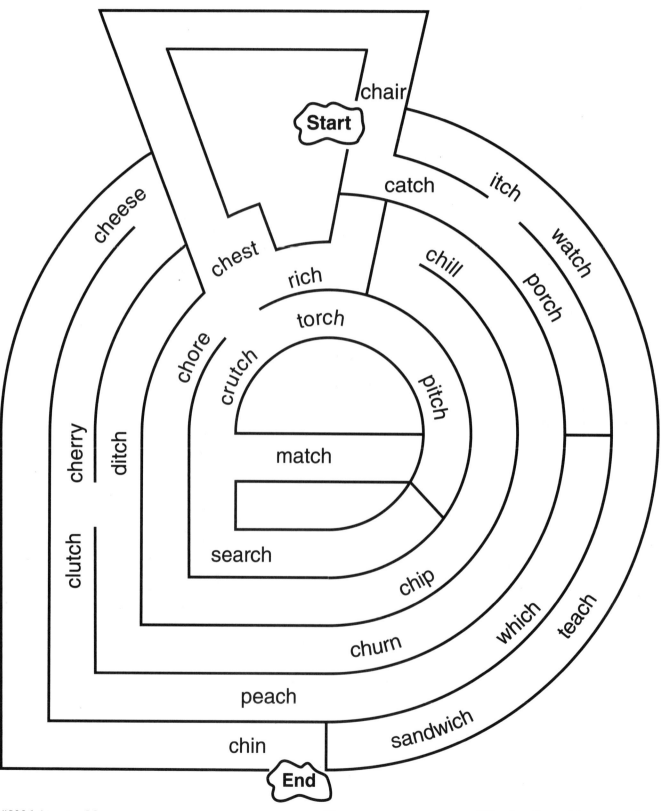

Letter Group: THR

Directions: Read each word. Follow the path of the words that begin with the *THR* sound as in *throng*.

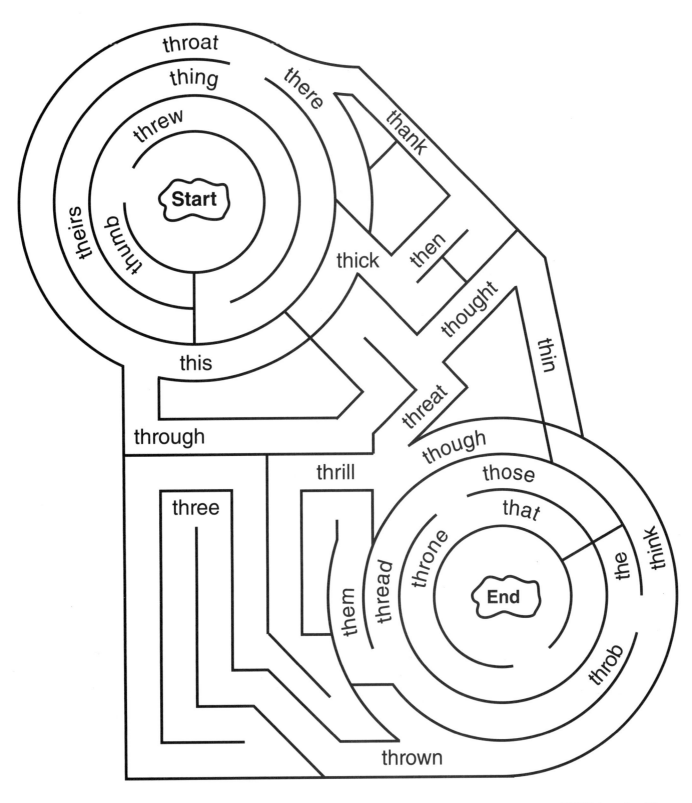

Color Words

Directions: Read each word. Follow the path of the words that are colors, such as *gold*.

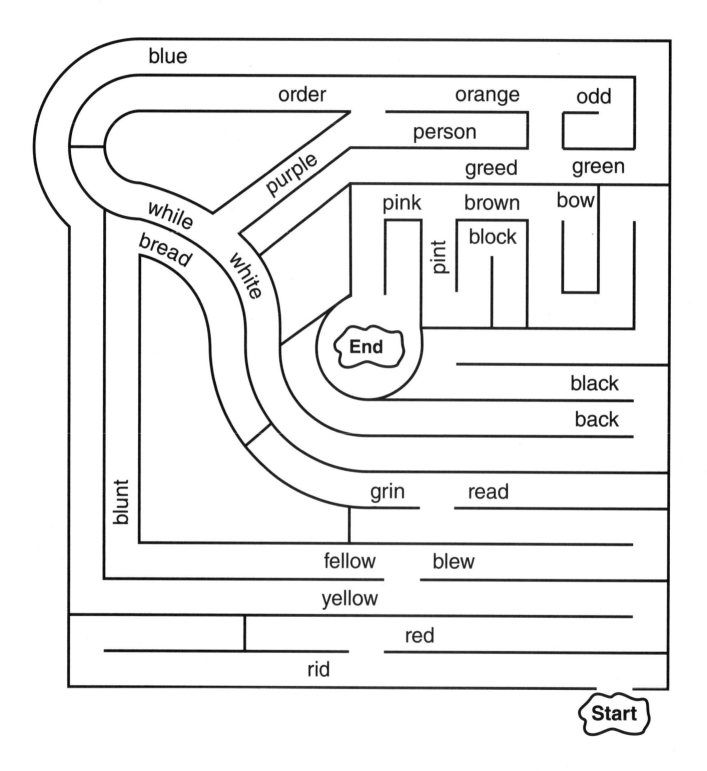

blue

order   orange   odd

person

purple   greed   green

while   pink   brown   bow

bread   white   pint   block

End

black

back

blunt   grin   read

fellow   blew

yellow

red

rid

Start

Number Words

Directions: Read each word. Follow the path of the words that are numbers, such as *zero*.

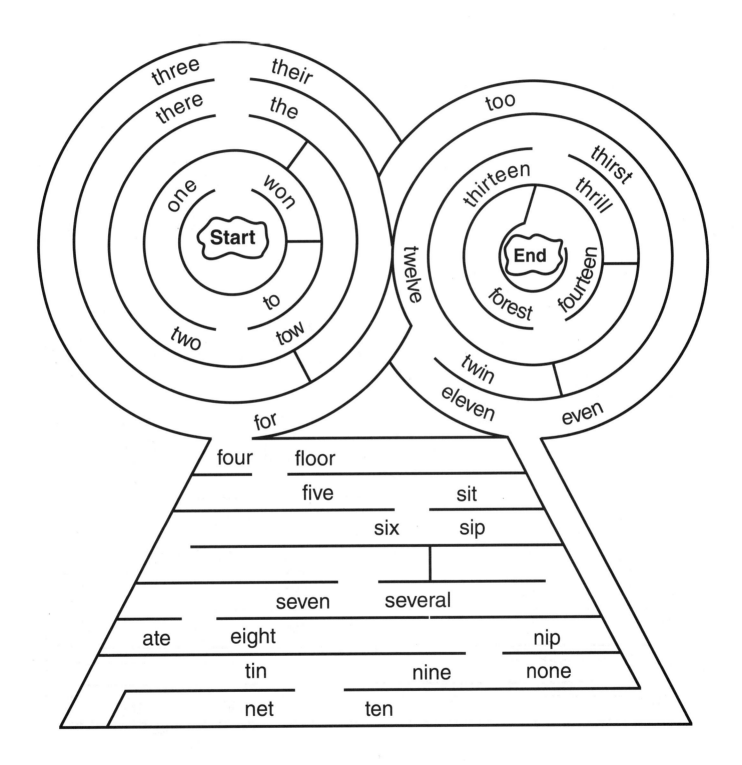

Size Words

Directions: Read each word. Follow the path of the words that tell a size, such as *smaller*.

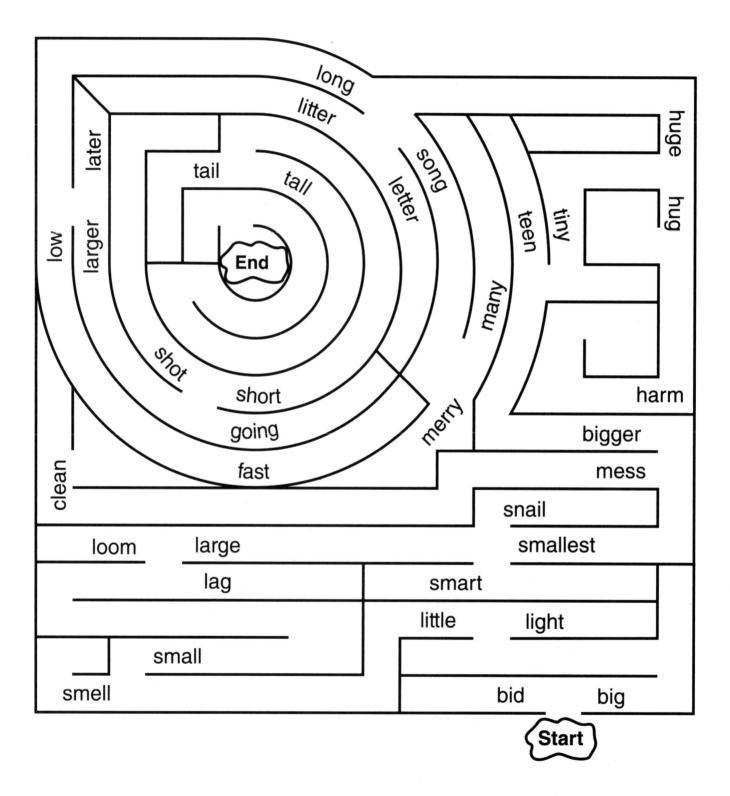

Family Words

Directions: Read each word. Follow the path of the words that name a family member, such as *mom*.

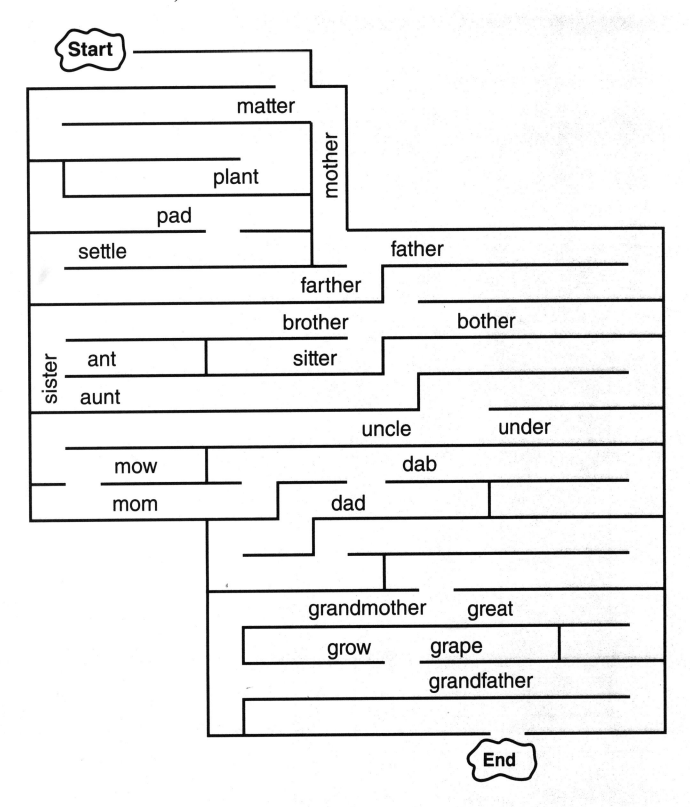

Start

matter

mother

plant

pad

settle   father

farther

brother   bother

sister ant   sitter

aunt

uncle   under

mow   dab

mom   dad

grandmother   great

grow   grape

grandfather

End

Animal Words

Directions: Read each word. Follow the path of the words that name an animal, such as *hog*.

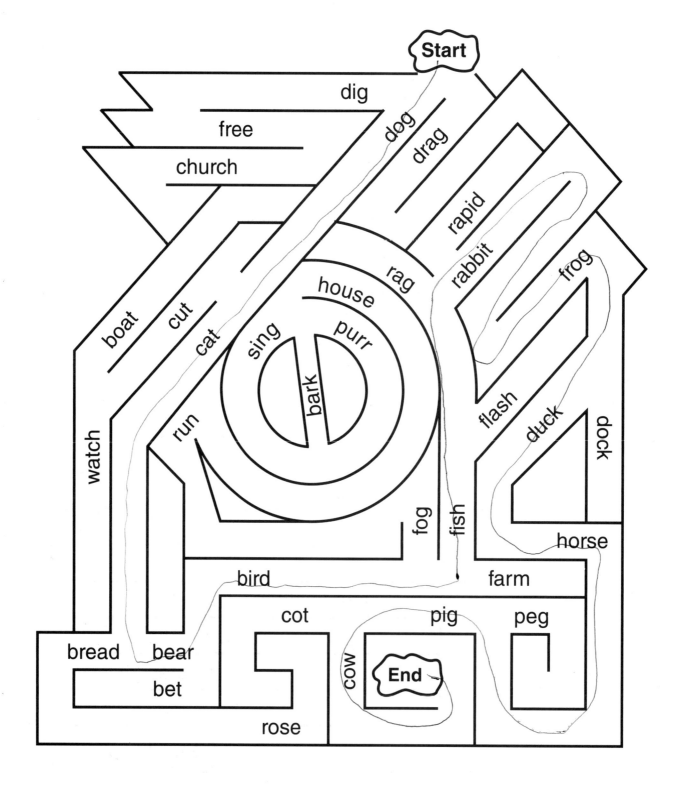

Weather Words

Directions: Read each word. Follow the path of the words about weather, such as *warm*.

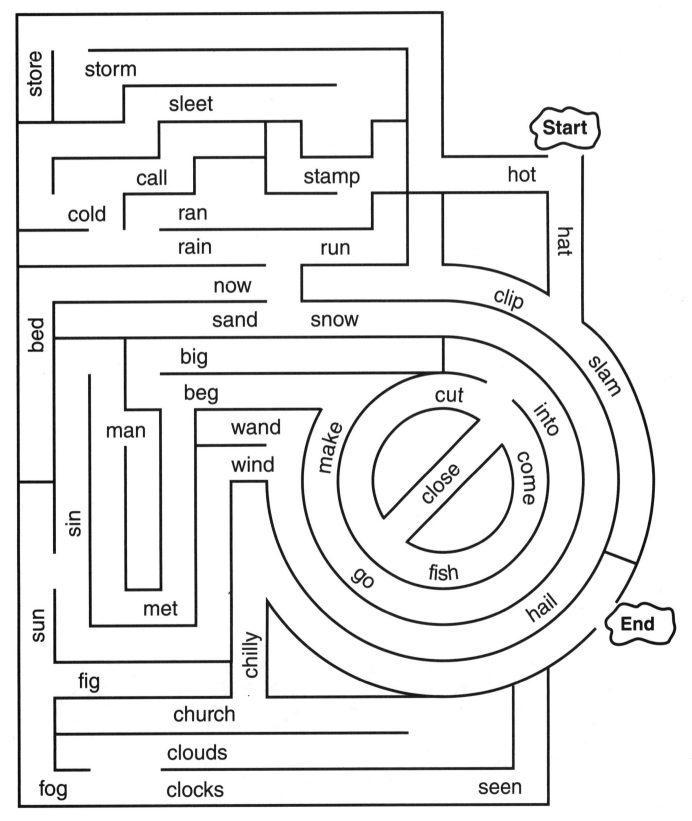

store

storm

sleet

Start

call   stamp   hot

cold   ran   hat

rain   run   clip

now   slam

bed   sand   snow

big   into

beg   cut   come

man   wand   make

wind   close

sin   End

sun   met   go   fish   hail

chilly

fig

church

clouds

fog   clocks   seen

Doing Words

Directions: Read each word. Follow the path of the words that tell something you can do, such as *kick*.

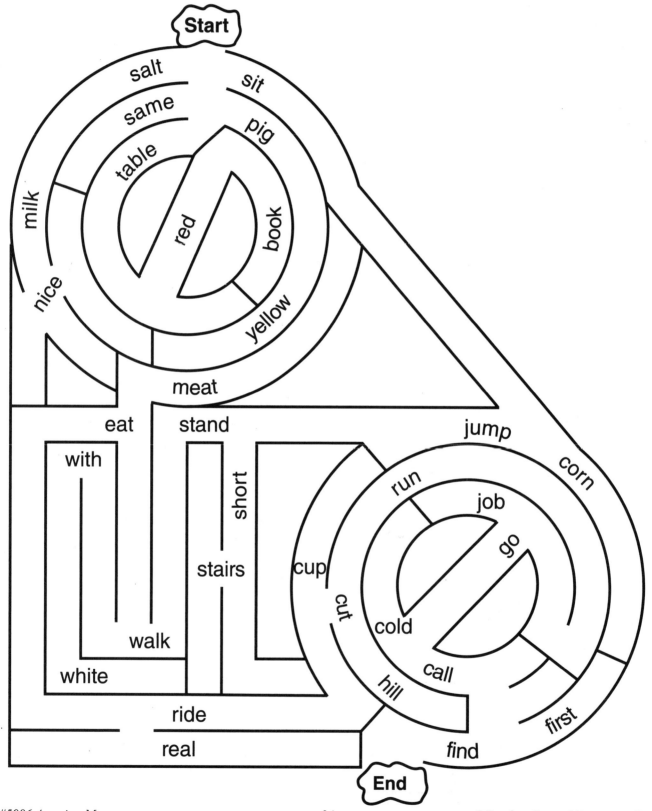

School Words

Directions: Read each word. Follow the path of the words that name something you see in school, such as *flag*.

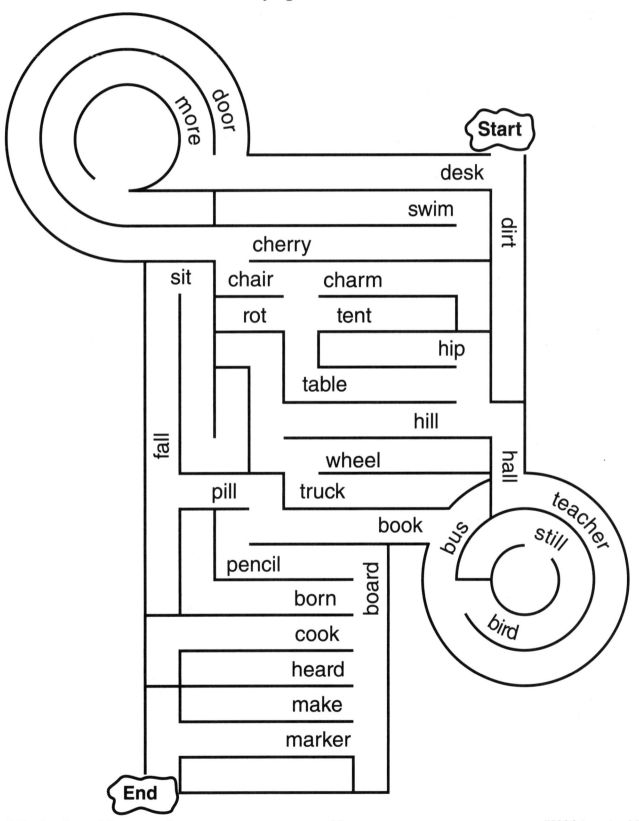

more

door

Start

desk

swim

cherry

sit

chair   charm

rot   tent

hip

table

dirt

hill

fall

wheel

hall

pill   truck

teacher

book

bus   still

pencil

born

board

bird

cook

heard

make

marker

End

Clothing Words

Directions: Read each word. Follow the path of the words that name something a person can wear, such as *cap*.

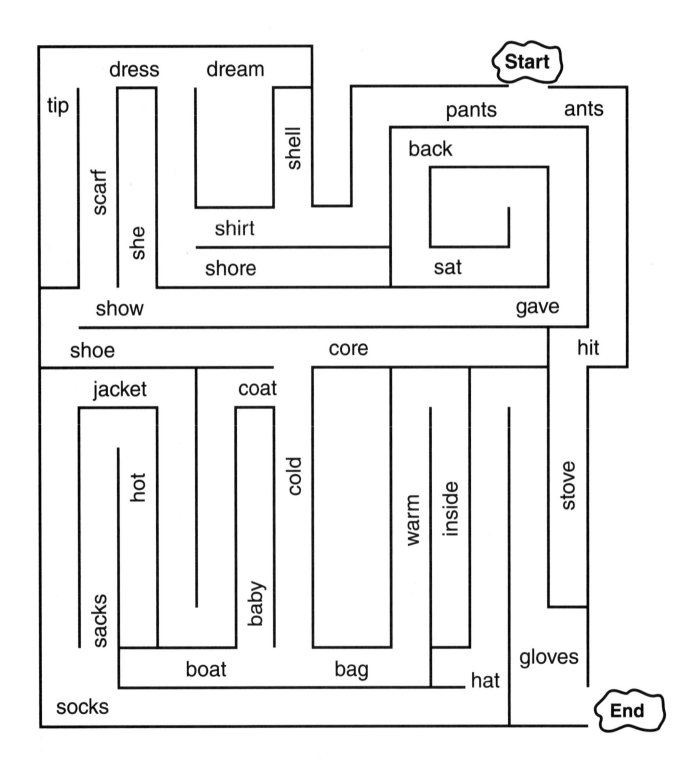

Food Words

Directions: Read each word. Follow the path of the words that name a food, such as *corn*, or a beverage, such as *tea*.

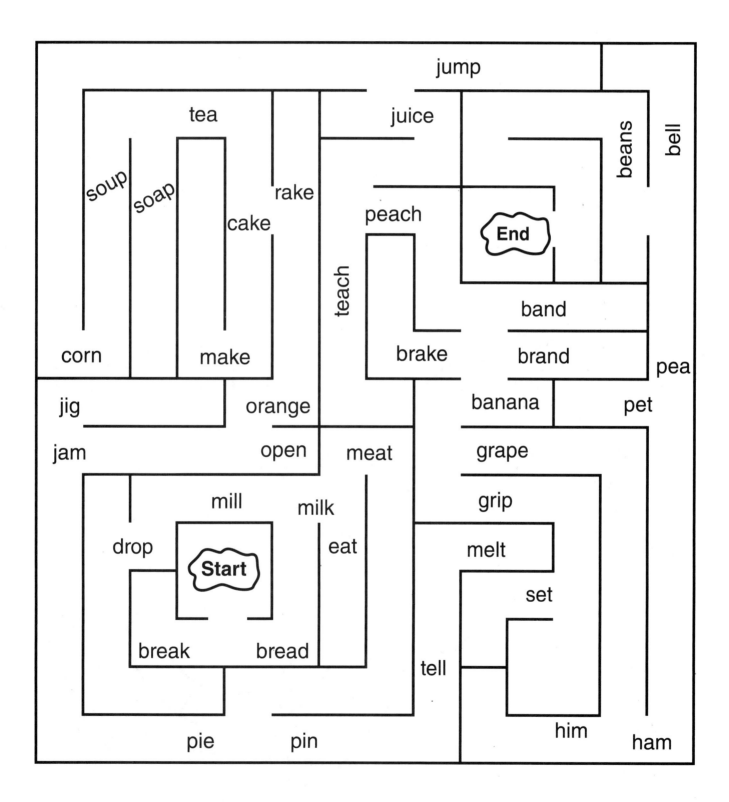

jump

tea   juice   beans   bell

soup   soap   rake   peach   **End**

cake   teach   band

corn   make   brake   brand   pea

jig   orange   banana   pet

jam   open   meat   grape

mill   milk   grip

drop   **Start**   eat   melt

set

break   bread   tell

pie   pin   him   ham

Place Words

Directions: Read each word. Follow the path of the words that name a place, such as *village*.

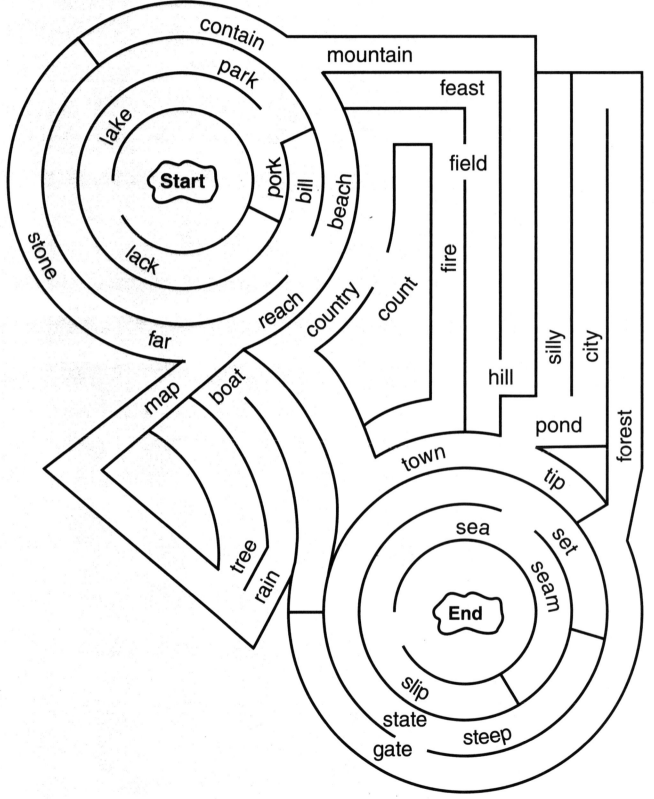

Car Words

Directions: Read each word. Follow the path of the words that name parts of a car, such as *hood*.

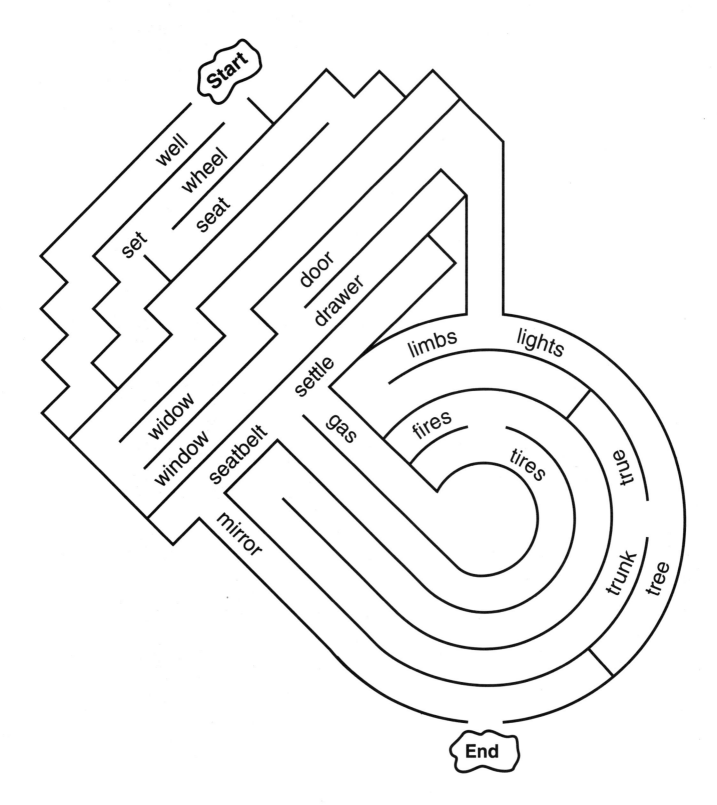

Counting Up by 2s

Directions: Follow the path of numbers that count up by 2s.

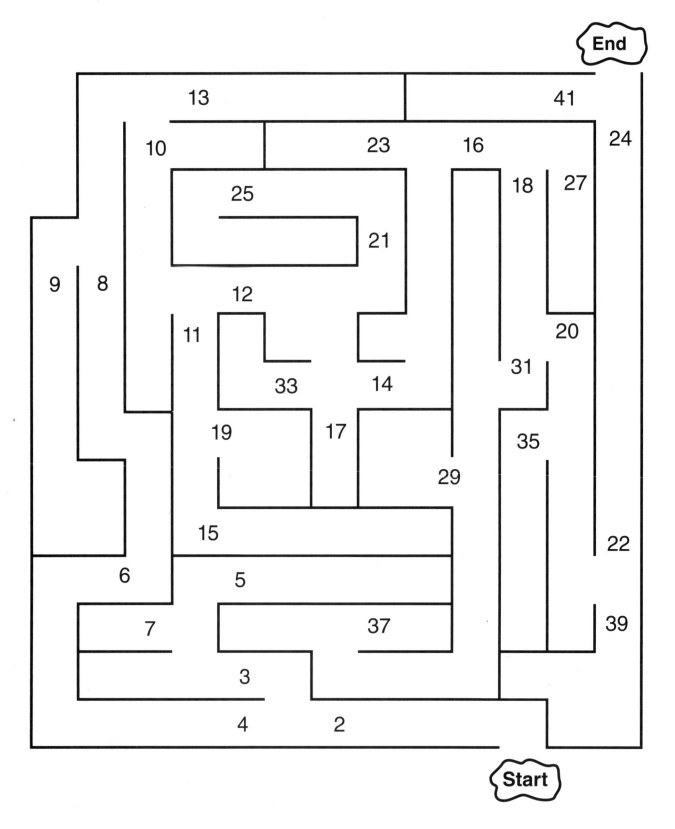

Counting Up by 5s

Directions: Follow the path of numbers that count up by 5s.

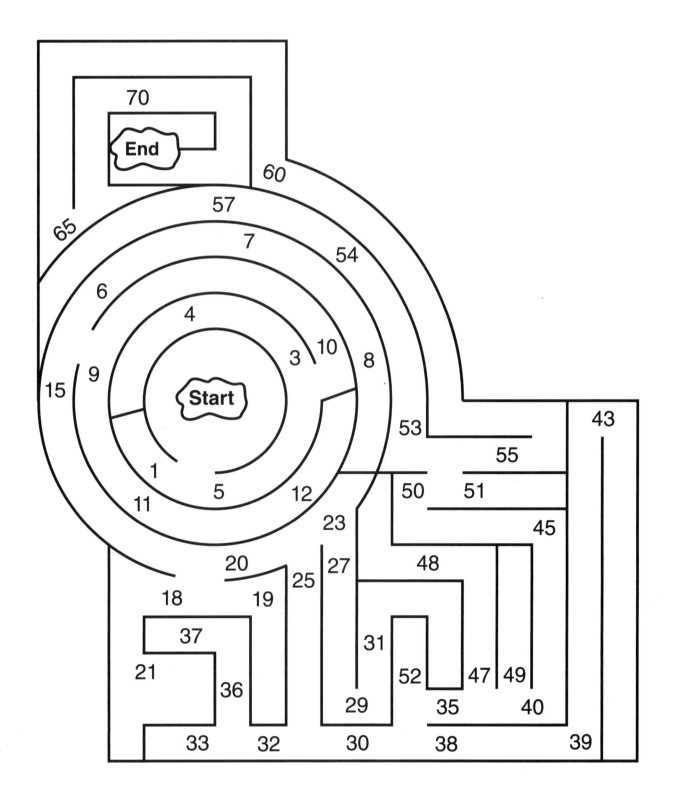

Counting Up by 10s

Directions: Follow the path of numbers that count up by 10s.

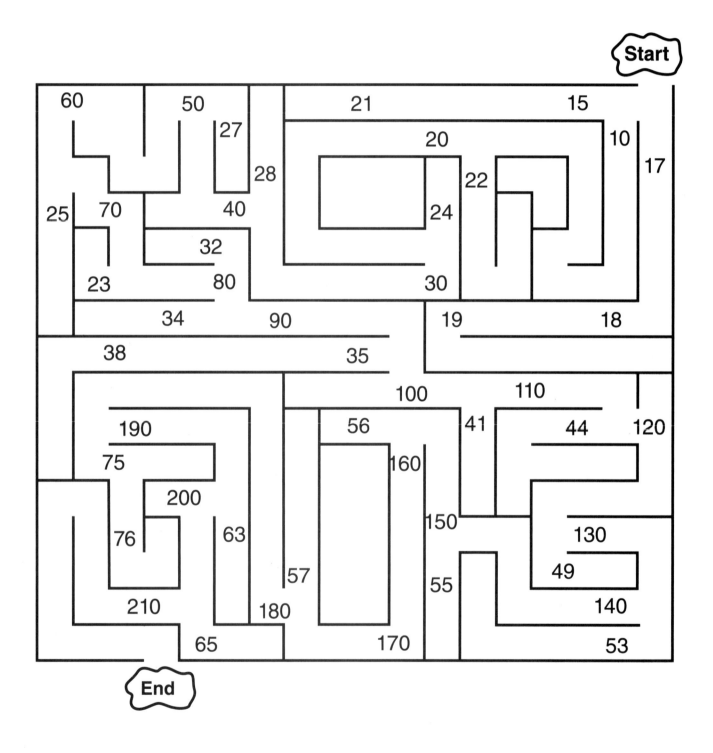

32

Ordinal Numbers

Directions: Ordinal numbers come in a series. We use them to put things in order, such as 1st, 2nd, 3rd, and 4th. Follow the path of ordinal numbers.

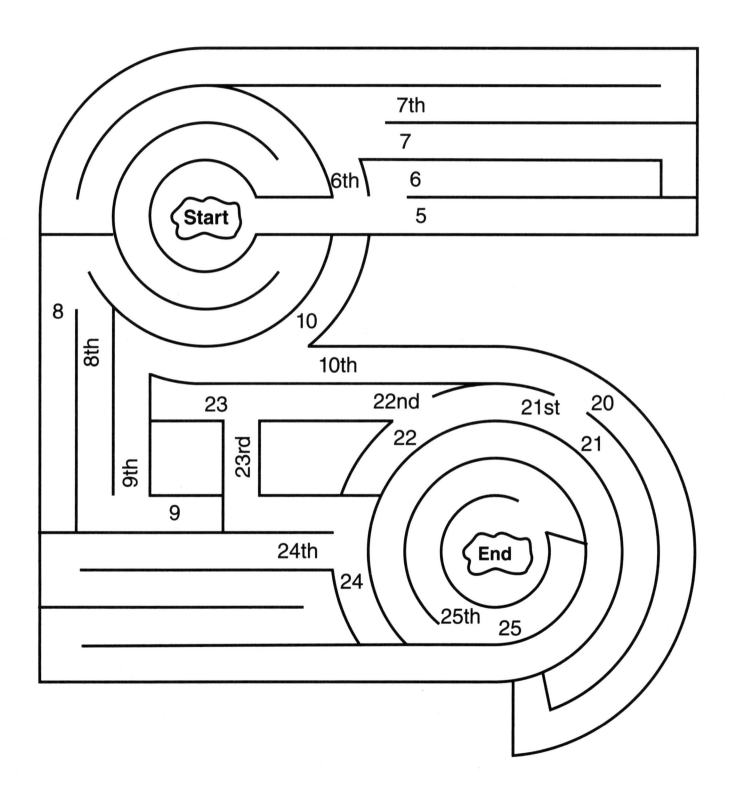

Odd Numbers

Directions: Follow the path of odd numbers.

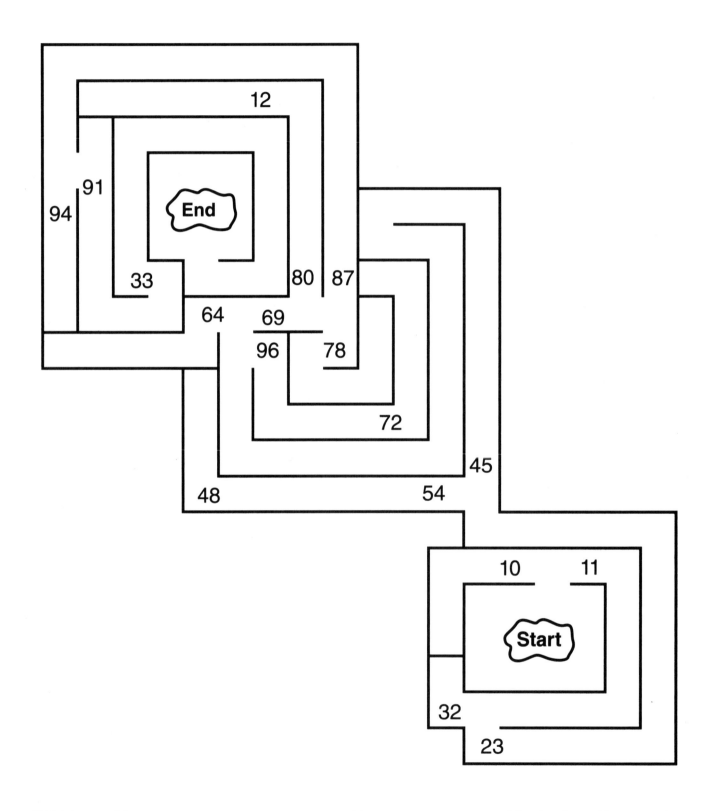

Even Numbers

Directions: Follow the path of even numbers.

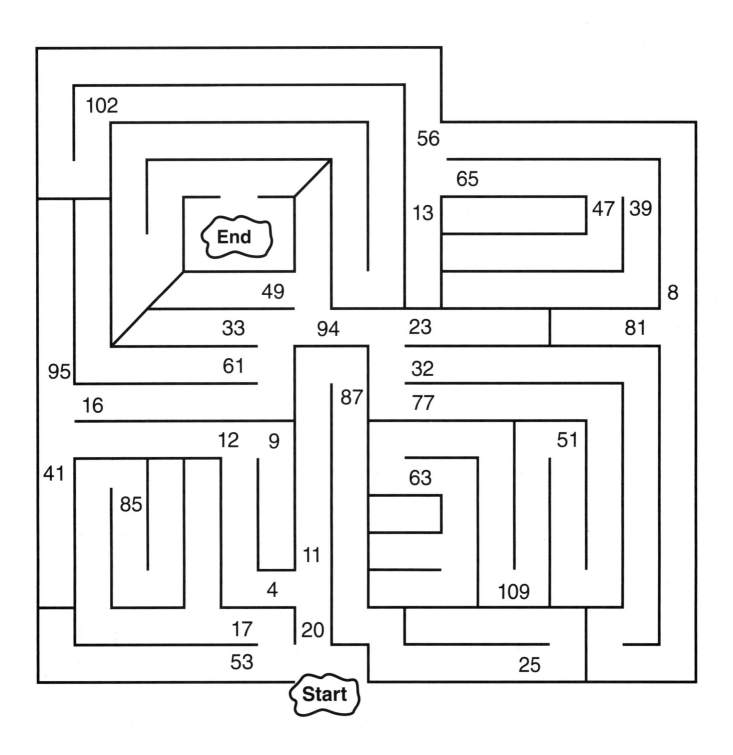

Largest Numbers

Directions: As you come to each choice, pick the path with the biggest number.

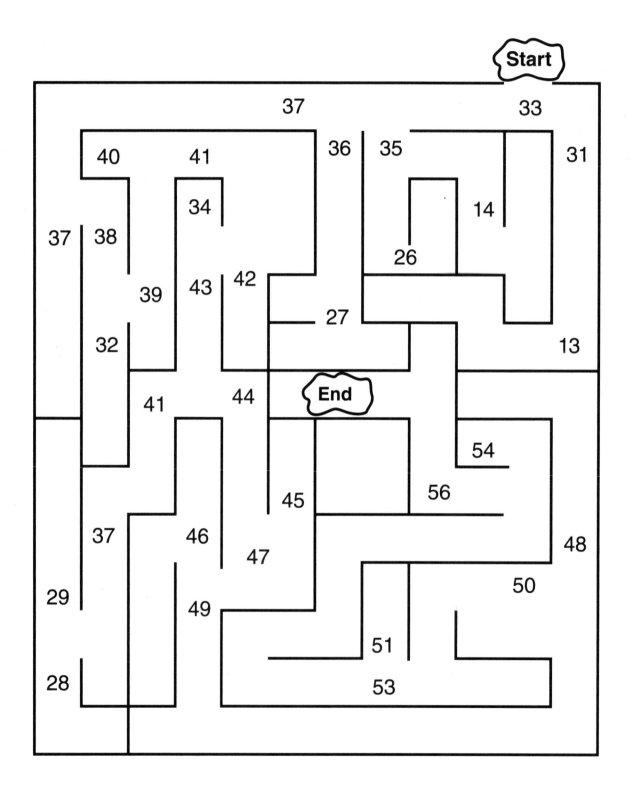

Smaller Numbers

Directions: As you come to each choice, pick the path with the smaller number.

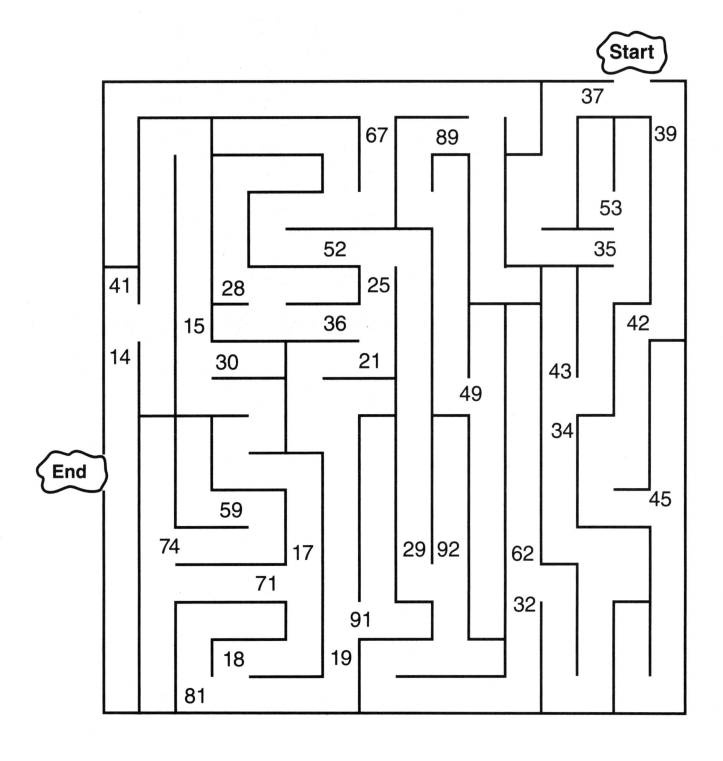

Numbers Greater Than

Directions: Follow the path of numbers that are greater than (more than) 63.

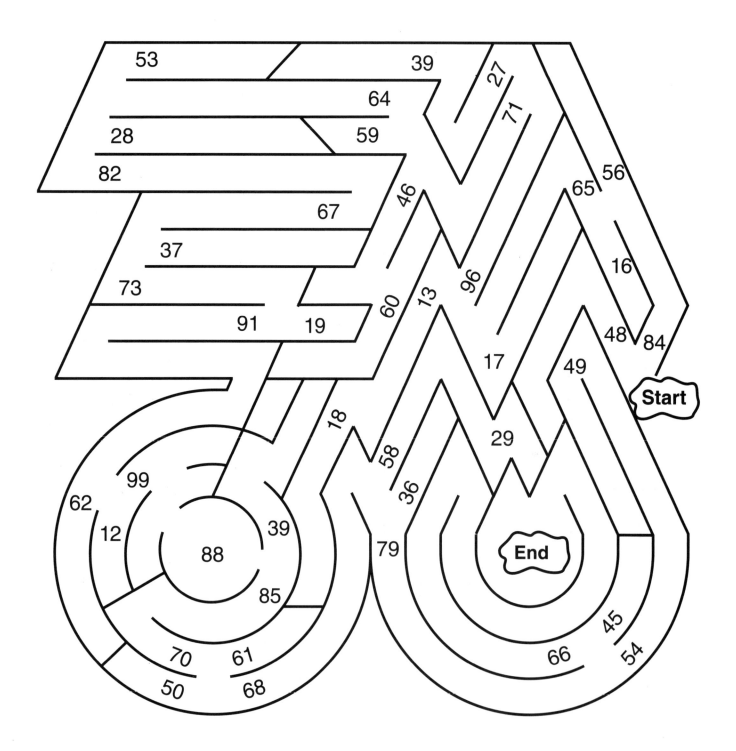

Numbers More Than

Directions: Follow the path of subtraction facts with answers that are more than (greater than) the answer to 10 − 2.

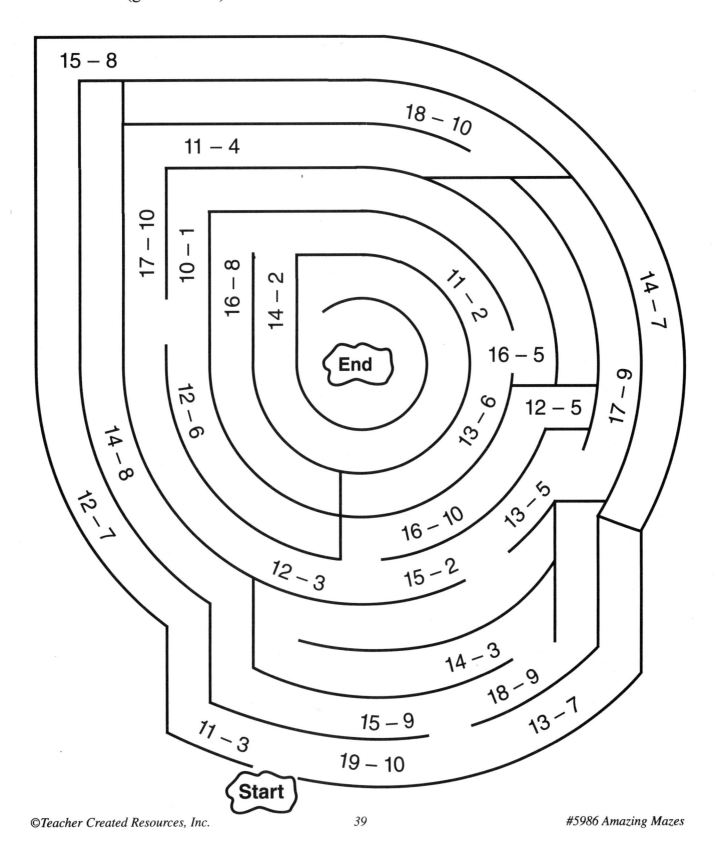

Numbers Less Than

Directions: Follow the path of subtraction facts with answers less than (smaller than) the answer to $15 - 3$.

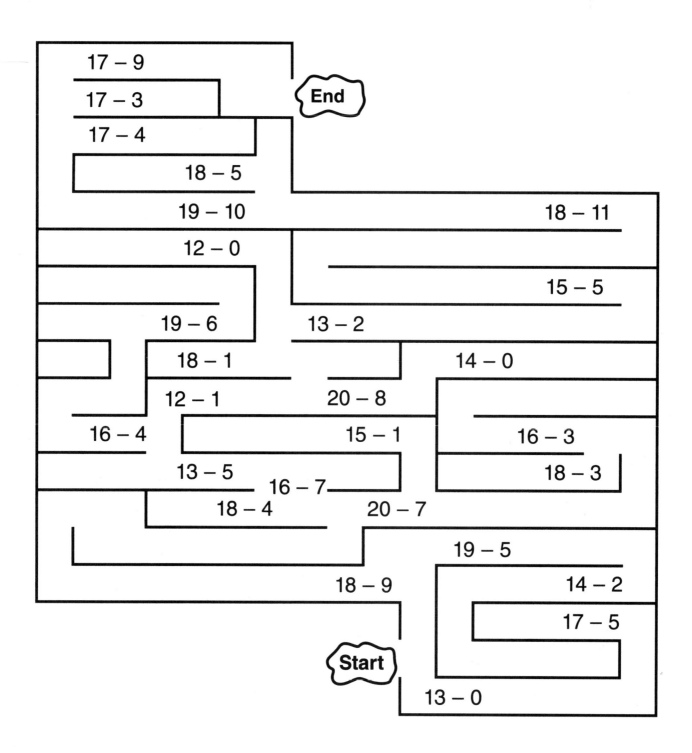

17 – 9

17 – 3

17 – 4

18 – 5

19 – 10

18 – 11

12 – 0

15 – 5

19 – 6

13 – 2

18 – 1

14 – 0

12 – 1

20 – 8

16 – 4

15 – 1

16 – 3

13 – 5

18 – 3

16 – 7

18 – 4

20 – 7

19 – 5

18 – 9

14 – 2

17 – 5

Start

13 – 0

End

Addition Facts that Equal 13

Directions: Follow the path of addition facts that equal 13.

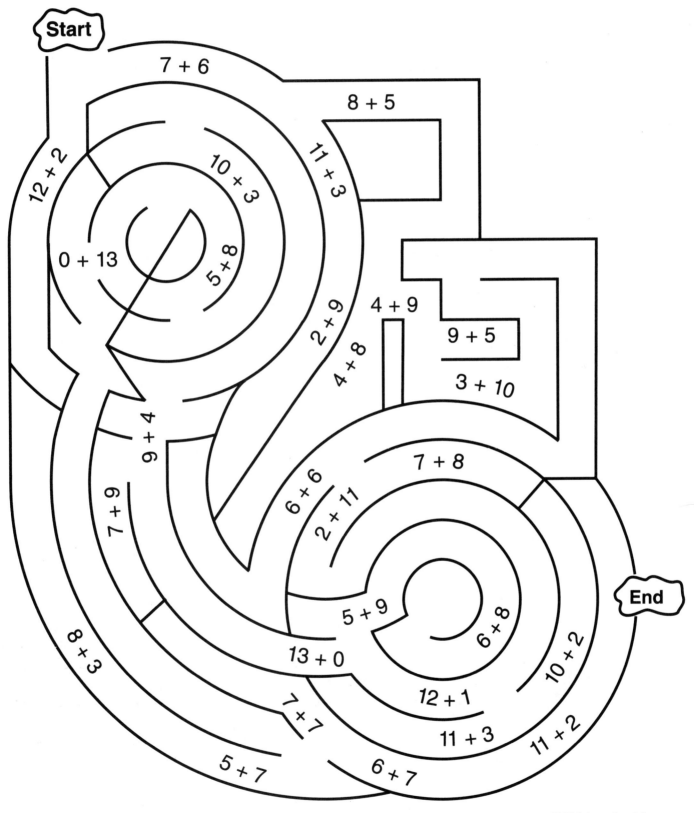

#5986 Amazing Mazes

Addition Facts that Equal 17

Directions: Follow the path of addition facts that equal 17.

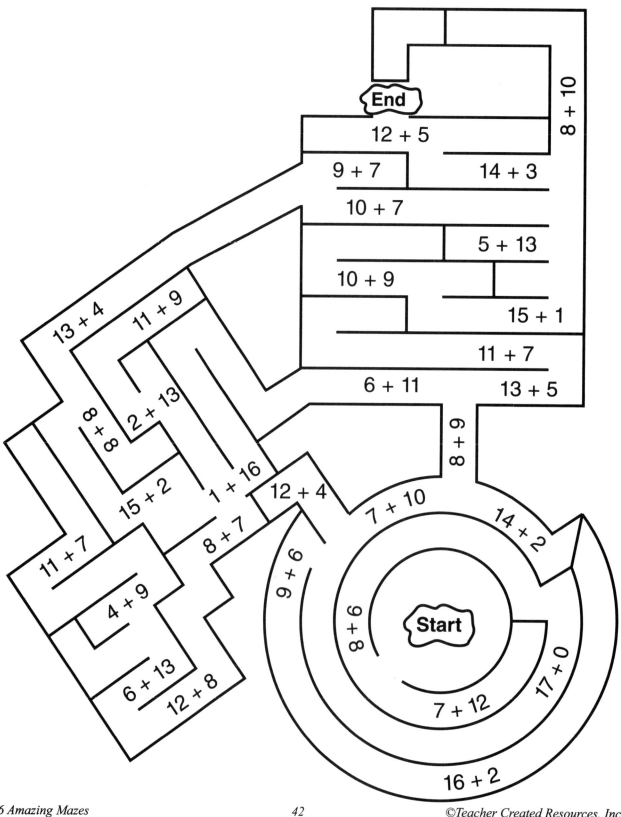

Addition Facts that Equal 19

Directions: Follow the path of addition facts that equal 19.

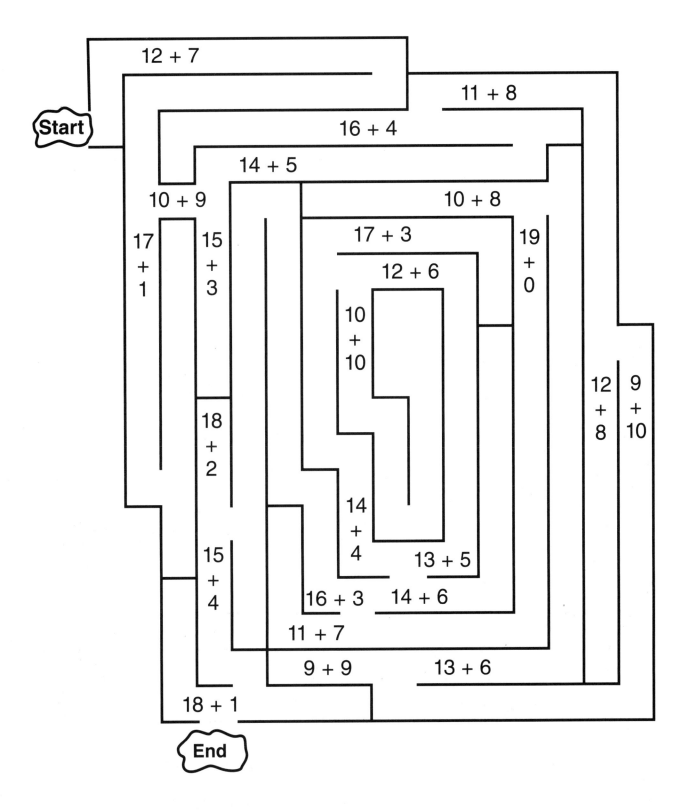

Subtraction Facts that Result in 4

Directions: Follow the path of subtraction facts that have an answer of 4.

Start

14 − 9	
9 − 4	6 − 2
12 − 5	8 − 4

11 − 7

5 − 2   13 − 8

7 − 4

12 − 6   7 − 3

10 − 5   8 − 5   11 − 6

5 − 1   12 − 8

4 − 0

10 − 6   6 − 4

6 − 3

9 − 5

14 − 10   11 − 8   6 − 1

10 − 4   13 − 9

10 − 7

15 − 11

End

44

Subtraction Facts that Result in 7

Directions: Follow the path of subtraction facts that have an answer of 7.

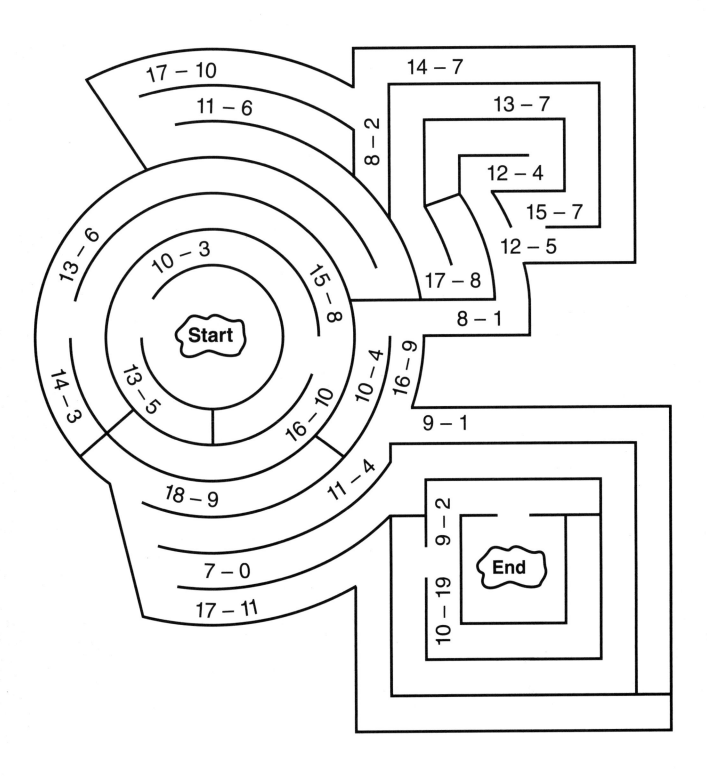

Subtraction Facts that Result in 9

Directions: Follow the path of subtraction facts that have an answer of 9.

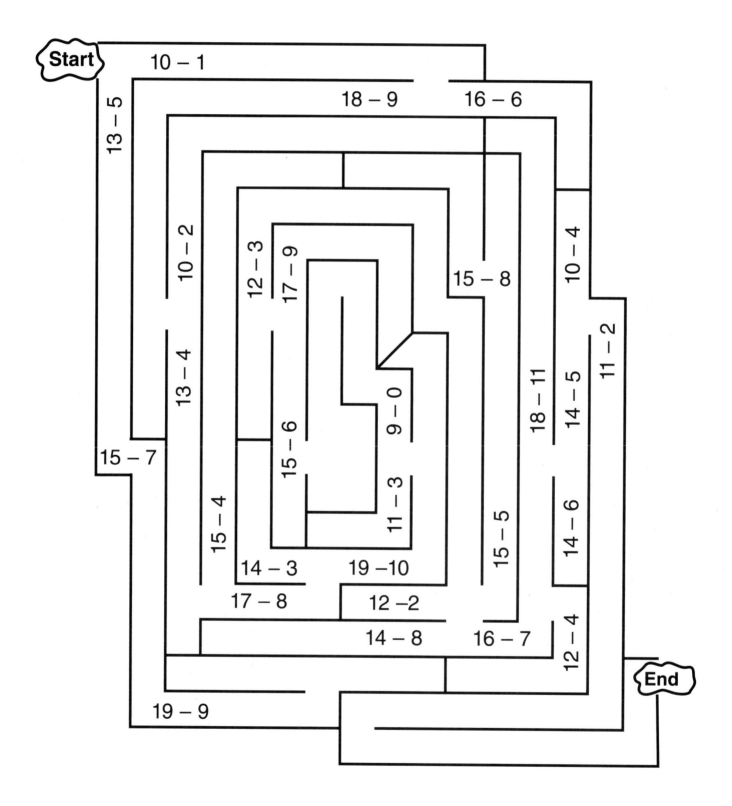

Start

10 – 1

18 – 9   16 – 6

13 – 5

10 – 2

12 – 3   17 – 9   15 – 8   10 – 4

13 – 4

9 – 0   11 – 2

15 – 7   18 – 11   14 – 5

15 – 6

15 – 4   11 – 3

14 – 3   19 –10   15 – 5   14 – 6

17 – 8   12 –2

14 – 8   16 – 7   12 – 4

19 – 9   **End**

More Money: Cents

Directions: Cents can be shown with a ¢ symbol or a $ symbol. So, 45¢ is the same as $0.45. There are no dollars and 45 cents. As you come to each choice, pick the path that has the most cents.

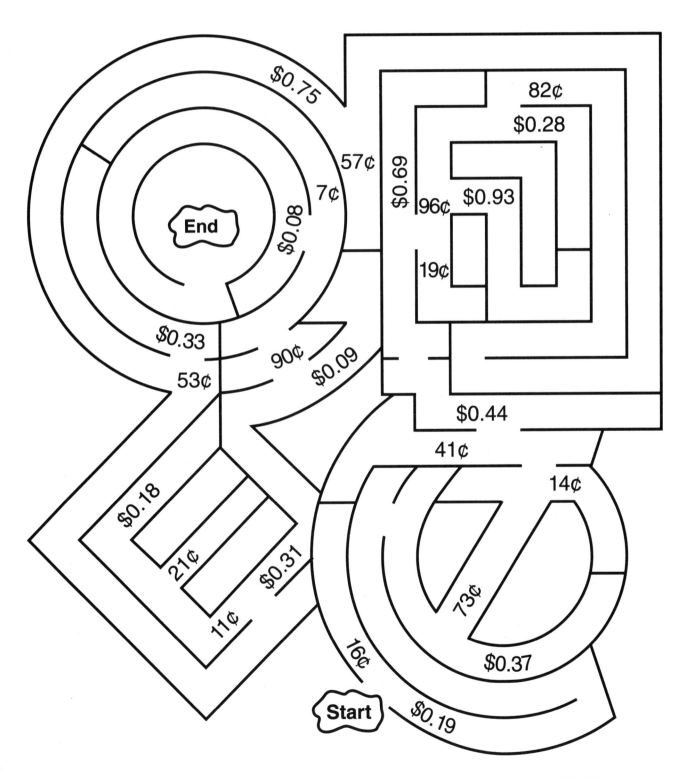

More Money: Dollars

Directions: As you come to each choice, pick the path with the most dollars.

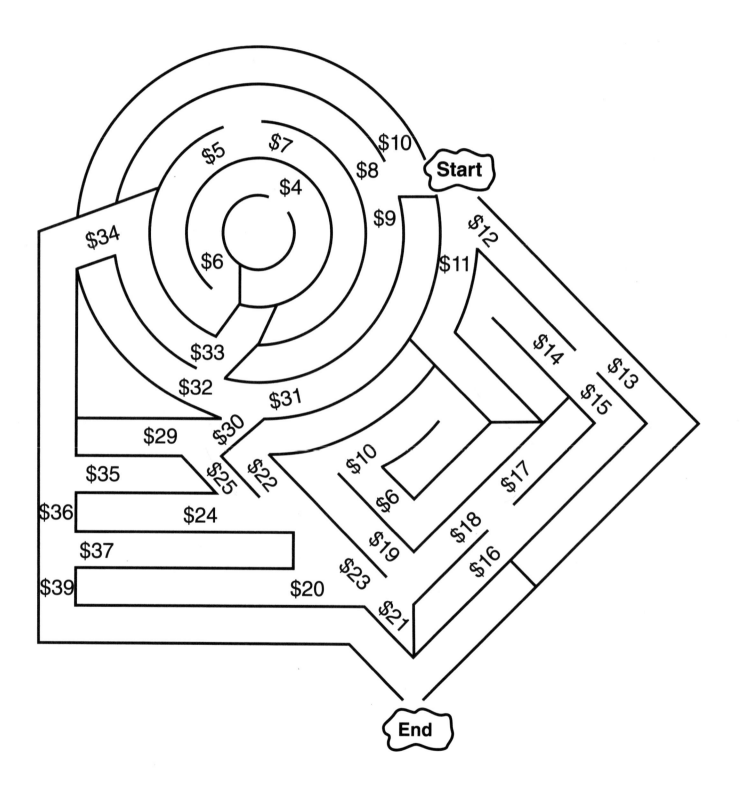

More Money: Dollars & Cents

Directions: As you come to each choice, pick the path with more money.

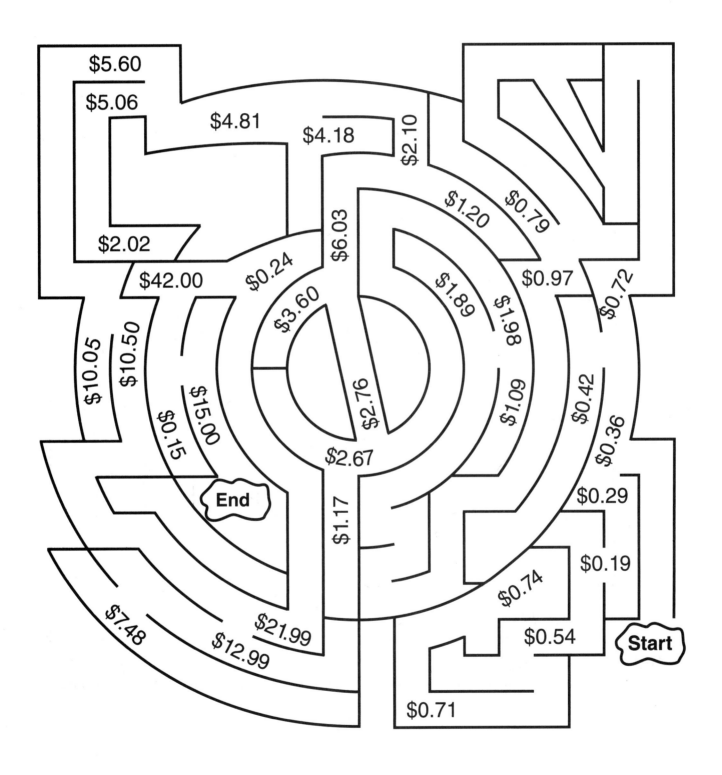

Less Money: Cents

Directions: Cents can be shown with a ¢ symbol or a $ symbol. So, 64¢ is the same as $0.64. There are no dollars and 64 cents. As you come to each choice, pick the path that has the fewest (least) cents.

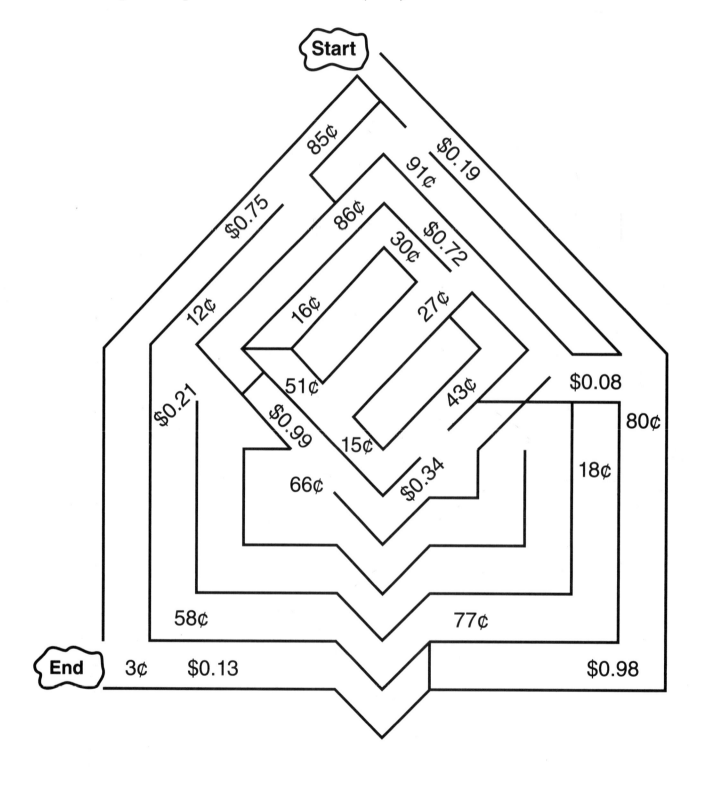

Start

85¢

$0.19

91¢

$0.75

86¢

$0.72

30¢

12¢

16¢

27¢

51¢

$0.08

$0.21

43¢

80¢

$0.99

15¢

18¢

66¢

$0.34

58¢

77¢

End

3¢ $0.13

$0.98

50

Less Money: Dollars

Directions: As you come to each choice, pick the path with the fewest (least) dollars.

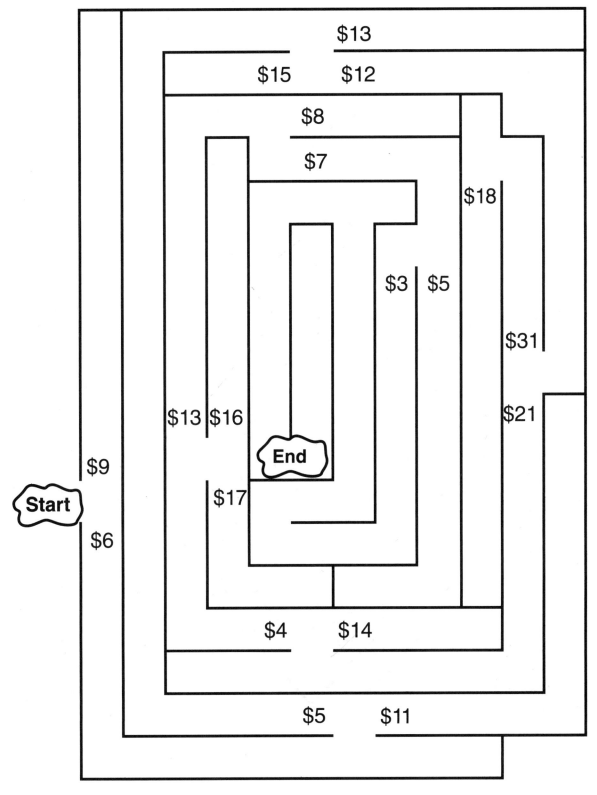

Less Money: Dollars & Cents

Directions: As you come to each choice, pick the path with the least amount of money.

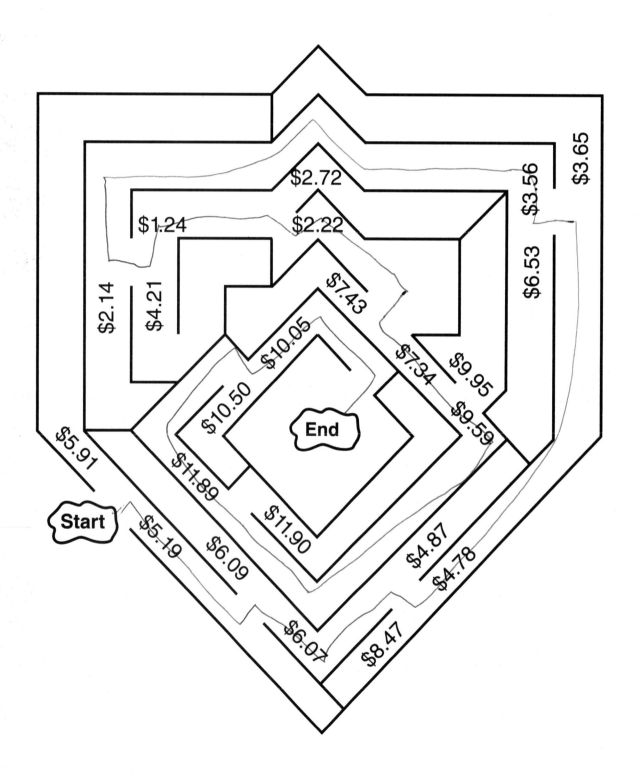

Days of the Week

Directions: Follow the path of the days of the week in order.

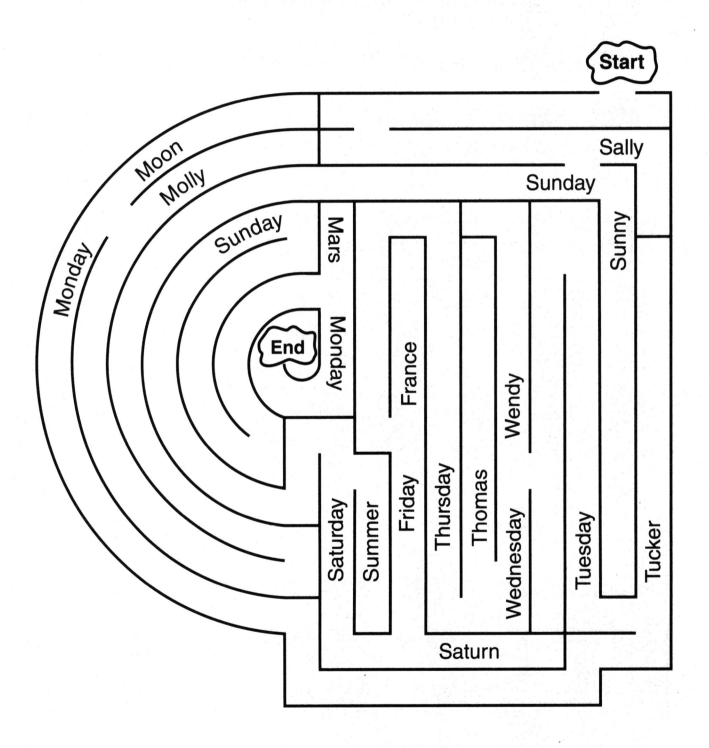

Months

Directions: Follow the path of the months of the year in order.

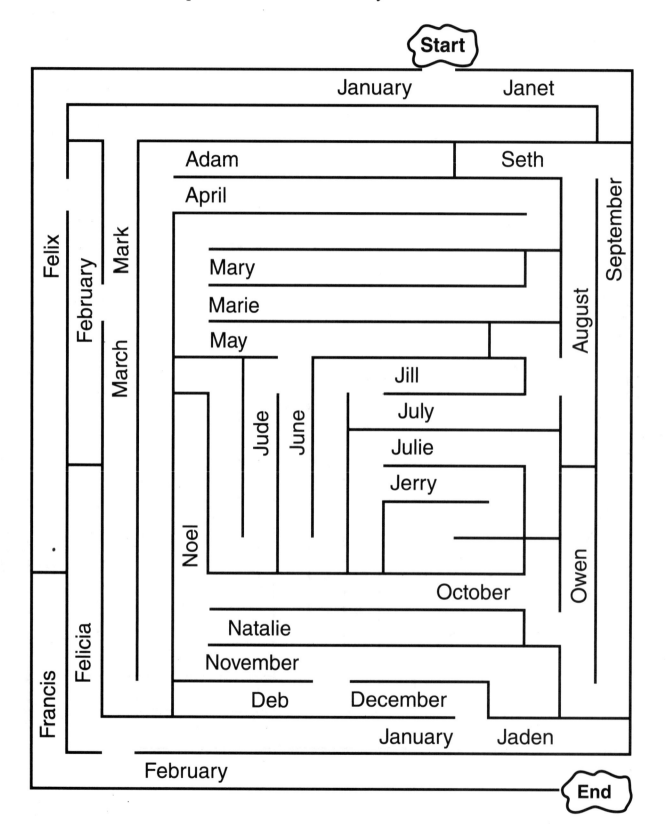

Relative Time

Directions: As you come to each choice, pick the time that is shortest (least).

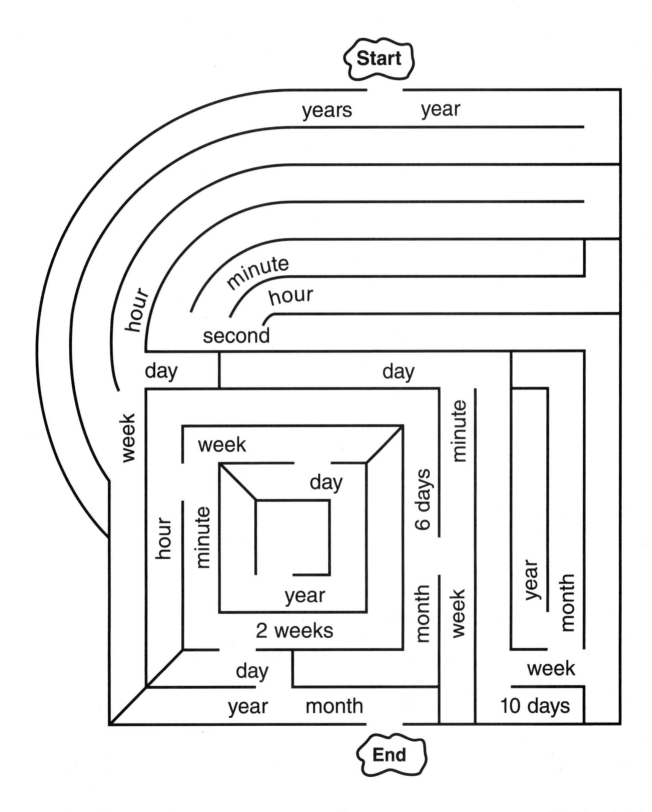

Answer Key

Short A, page 4

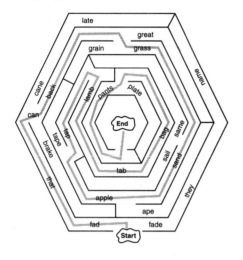

Long A, page 5

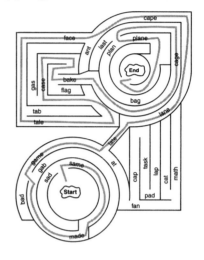

Short E, page 6

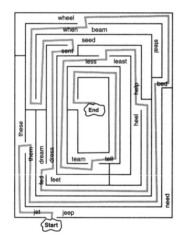

Long E, page 7

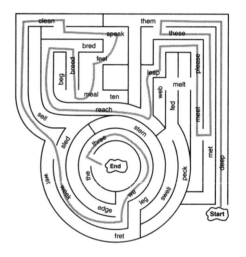

Short I, page 8

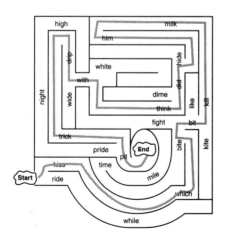

Long I, page 9

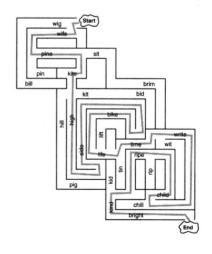

Answer Key *(cont.)*

Short O, page 10

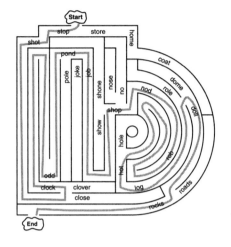

Long O, page 11

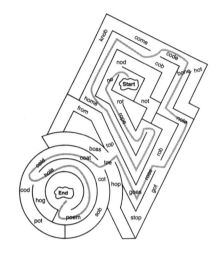

Short U, page 12

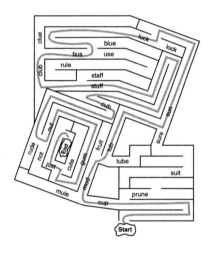

Long U, page 13

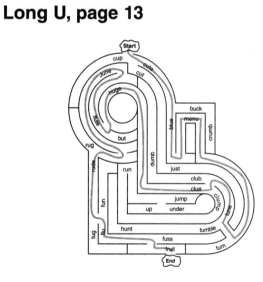

Y is a Consonant, page 14

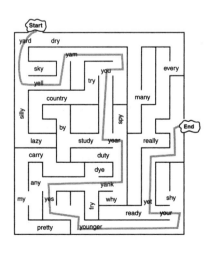

Y is a Vowel, page 15

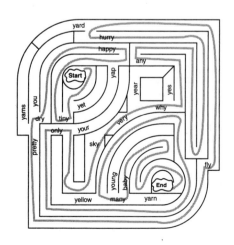

Answer Key *(cont.)*

Letter Pair: CH, page 16

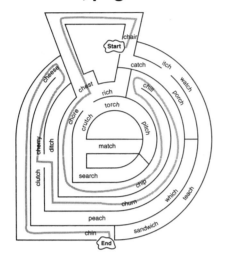

Letter Group: THR, page 17

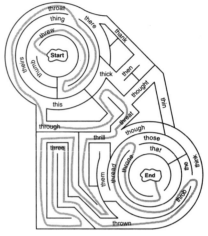

Color Words, page 18

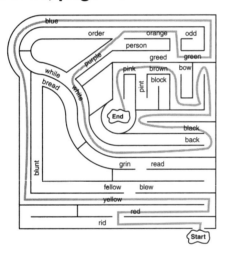

Number Words, page 19

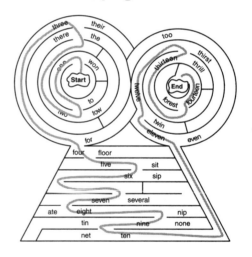

Size Words, page 20

Family Words, page 21

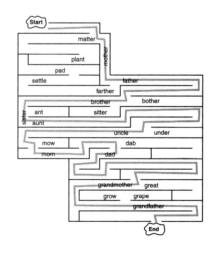

Answer Key *(cont.)*

Animal Words, page 22

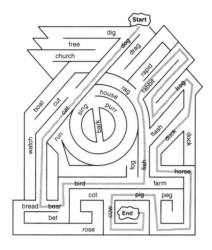

Weather Words, page 23

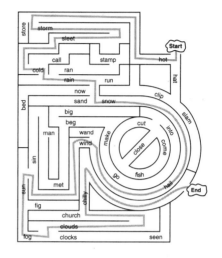

Doing Words, page 24

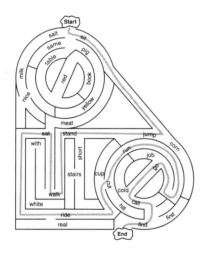

School Words, page 25

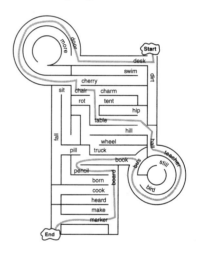

Clothing Words, page 26

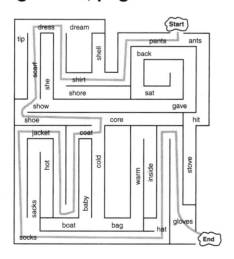

Food Words, page 27

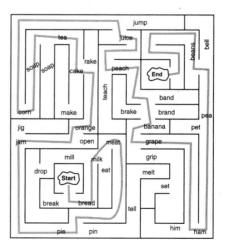

Answer Key *(cont.)*

Place Words, page 28

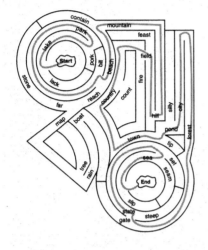

Car Words, page 29

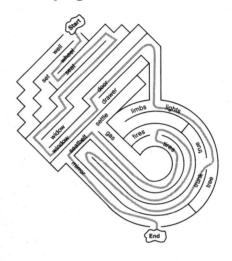

Counting Up by 2s, page 30

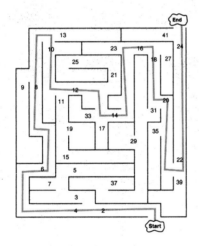

Counting Up by 5s, page 31

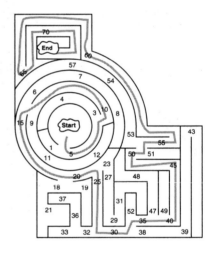

Counting Up by 10s, page 32

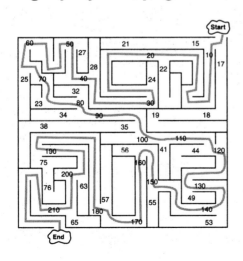

Ordinal Numbers, page 33

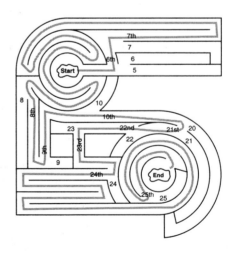

Answer Key *(cont.)*

Odd Numbers, page 34

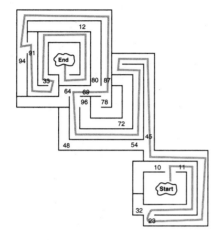

Even Numbers, page 35

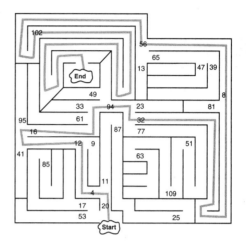

Larger Numbers, page 36

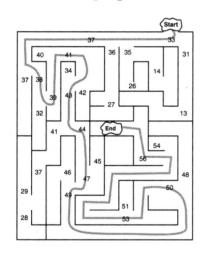

Smaller Numbers, page 37

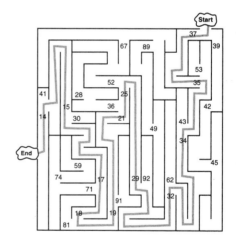

Numbers Greater Than, page 38

Numbers More Than, page 39

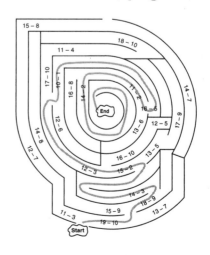

Answer Key *(cont.)*

Numbers Less Than, page 40

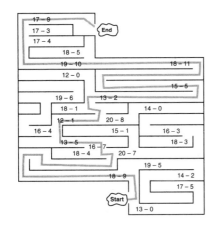

Addition Facts that Equal 13, page 41

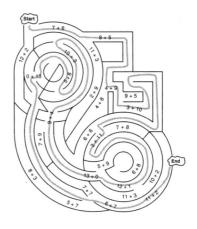

Addition Facts that Equal 17, page 42

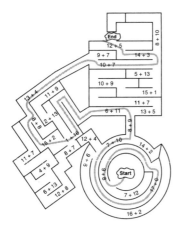

Addition Facts that Equal 19, page 43

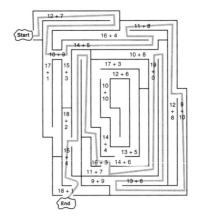

Subtraction Facts that Result in 4, page 44

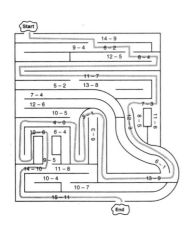

Subtraction Facts that Result in 7, page 45

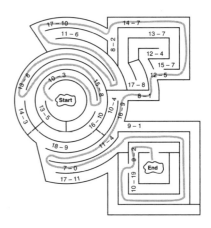

Answer Key *(cont.)*

Subtraction Facts that Result in 9, page 46

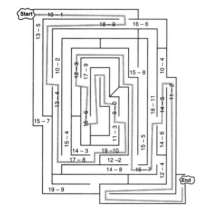

More Money: Cents, page 47

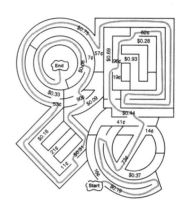

More Money: Dollars, page 48

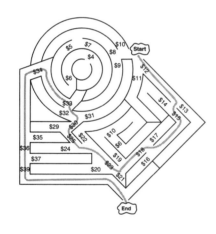

More Money: Dollars & Cents, page 49

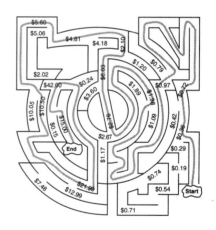

Less Money: Cents, page 50

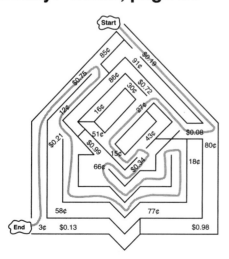

Less Money: Dollars, page 51

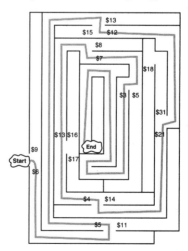

Answer Key *(cont.)*

Less Money: Dollars & Cents, page 52

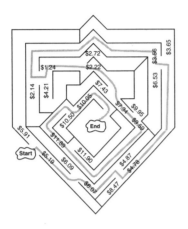

Days of the Week, page 53

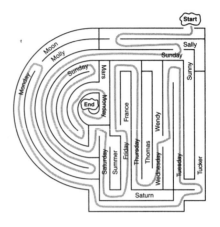

Months, page 54

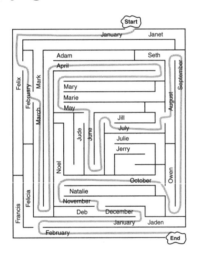

Relative Time, page 55

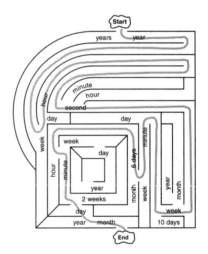